Global Mindedness in International Social Work Practice

Reshaping Social Work Series

Series Editors: Lena Dominelli and Malcolm Payne

The Reshaping Social Work series aims to develop the knowledge base for critical, reflective practitioners. Each book is designed to support students on qualifying social work programs and update practitioners on crucial issues in today's social work, strengthening research knowledge, critical analysis and skilled practice to shape social work to meet future challenges.

Published titles

Invitation to authors

The Series Editors welcome proposals for new books within the *Reshaping Social Work* series. Please contact one of the series editors for an initial discussion:

- Lena Dominelli at lena.dominelli@durham.ac.uk
- Malcolm Payne at macolmpayne5@gmail.com

Global Mindedness in International Social Work Practice

Janet Carter Anand and Chaitali Das

First published 2019 by
RED GLOBE PRESS

Red Globe Press in the UK is an imprint of Springer Nature Limited,
registered in England, company number 785998, of 4 Crinan Street,
London, N1 9XW.

Red Globe Press® is a registered trademark in the United States,
the United Kingdom, Europe and other countries.

ISBN 978–1–137–36208–7 paperback

This book is printed on paper suitable for recycling and made from fully
managed and sustained forest sources. Logging, pulping and manufacturing
processes are expected to conform to the environmental regulations of the
country of origin.

A catalogue record for this book is available from the British Library.

A catalog record for this book is available from the Library of Congress.

This book is dedicated to Karan and Oliver

Contents

1 International Social Work – the Vision and the Reality

Introduction

The reality that people's lives increasingly transcend national boundaries, and that global events shape local lives, has led to the recognition that the scope of social work is international in scale. Social work problems and solutions are no longer located and contained within local or national boundaries. International social work, in this context, has increasingly gained importance in response to developments that go beyond national confines. The concept of international social work and its relevance for human rights has therefore gained currency.

Despite the number of publications and courses on 'International social work' the concept itself remains difficult to define. The confusion relates to the different ideas, approaches and orientations attributed to the term. Midgley (1990) suggested that international social work is a 'broad umbrella term referring to any aspect of social work involving two or more nations' and emphasised the idea of nations working in partnership. Healy (2001) defines international social work as all social work that may require international knowledge. Dominelli (2004a), Ife (2010) and Akimoto (2008), however, highlight the importance of processes and consequences that globalisation has on social work and takes into account the need to consider the dialectical relationship between the local and the global. In this book, we also argue that international social work is a way of thinking about social work based on a critical understanding of the interplay between local problems and global issues that pervades practice.

This book acknowledges the importance of a global approach to the profession and attempts to develop this further by presenting global mindedness as an approach for transformative practice. The notion of global mindedness in social work refers to the recognition and building upon the relationship between global and local contexts in day-to-day practice. The nature of this relationship, though acknowledged in academic circles, remains understated in social work education and practice. The relevance of global issues to local practice and the influence of local practice on global issues are not always apparent to students and practitioners.

In the following chapters, we outline our approach to global mindedness, its conceptualisation and operationalisation in practice. This exploration is undertaken by critically deconstructing and reconstructing how social issues are perceived and understood by social workers. We highlight the importance of going beyond one's own context to explore the diversities of human experience around the world, as the basis for transformative practice. Case studies are used extensively in the following chapters to encourage students, academics and practitioners to apply the values, knowledge and skills required for global mindedness to their own practice. We hope the case studies will also serve as useful pedagogical recources for educators that will enable them to bring both human rights and international social work issues into the classroom and foster discussion to unravel the relationship between the global and the local. This book adds a new perspective on international social work that is relevant and applicable to the day-to-day experiences of social work students, educators and practitioners. Since the concept of global mindedness builds on the literature on international social work, this chapter outlines the key debates of international social work. This chapter also highlights issues within globalisation that have a profound impact on international social work.

Defining International Social Work

There are many definitions of international social work. In 2014, the International Federation of Social Workers and the International Association of Social Workers further developed the definition of social work to represent the diverse traditions and cultures inherent in the profession. The following is the current definition internationally accepted by most schools of social work:

> Social work is a practice-based profession and an academic discipline that promotes *social change and development, social cohesion,* and the empowerment and liberation of people. Principles of social justice, human rights, *collective responsibility and respect for diversities* are central to social work. Underpinned by theories of social work, social sciences, *humanities and indigenous knowledge,* social work *engages people and structures to address life challenges and enhance wellbeing.* The above definition may be amplified at national and/or regional levels."
>
> (IFAW/IASSW, 2014)

Underlying this definition is an assumption that social workers share a common understanding as to the aims and vision for their professional practice. Hare (2004), Lorenz (2001) and Gray et al. (2012) have questioned whether a common international social work is achievable or desirable. The current definition incorporates diverse, if not contradictory, theoretical traditions ranging from conservative ambitions, such as the social cohesion of society, to radical aims, namely the liberation of people. In addition, a commitment to the humanities, social sciences and indigenous knowledge also implies tensions as to how knowledge production is prioritised. For example, how evidence-based social work as promoted in professional literature and pedagogy across the United Kingdom (UK) and Europe is reconciled with the development of forms of social work grounded in indigenous knowledge in countries such as New Zealand, Canada, Australia, the United States of America (USA), as well as in Latin American countries. Incorporating such different traditions of social work has made the current definition and perhaps all attempts at defining international social work problematic. Nevertheless, professional social work continues to seek a global definition, identity and status in recognition of its overarching commitment to support vulnerable too patronising people.

What then are the unifying elements within our understanding of international social work? To start with, social work involves the application of the definition of social work across 'international' fields. Healy (2001) provides a pragmatic conceptualisation of these fields to include four broad dimensions: impact of globalisation on social work practice, comparative enquiry, professional collaboration and exchange. Increasingly, these dimensions span across all aspects of social work where global trends intersect with local concerns. All social work, for example, is affected by the processes of globalisation (directly or indirectly) and social work increasingly deals with people who have transnational identities or cross borders. Ife (2008) suggests that the human rights framework can offer the profession a common perspective that is universally applicable. The centrality of human rights is convincing and appeals to social workers' desires to share a common aim. However, even the universality of human rights is not free from different interpretations; for example, the USA places emphasis on civil and political rights while Nordic countries such as Finland and Sweden place stress on collective, social and economic rights (Esping-Anderson, 1999). Most indigenous communities perceive environmental and land rights issues as a central component of their lives and livelihoods. It is clear that diverse orientations to human rights are shaped by the material, social, economic and political histories of these societies. The history of professional social work also highlights the different orientations of social work. An historical perspective is valuable in understanding the troubled relationships between internationalisation in general and the internationalisation of the profession including the opportunities and mistakes experienced. We explore this history briefly to uncover some of the key opportunities and limitations in international social work.

An Historical Understanding of International Social Work

The internationalisation of the social work profession is often talked about as if it were an entirely new concept, having little or no historical precedence. This is not the case. Social work began to assume a professional form in the late 19th century with the development of social work methods and practices which involved extensive international exchanges between the professionals in Europe (including the UK) and the USA (Gray et al., 2012). Social work ideology, practice and education were exported to other countries through colonial legal systems and welfare policies. A brief look at the history of social work highlights that it developed within an international space: through exchange of ideas between people in different places, influenced by events that were occurring across geographical areas beyond the confines of one single nation (Gray et al., 2012). The profession's development was both progressive and oppressive at the same time.

Western professional social work traces its development back to the 1800s in Europe and the USA. This was a period of social and economic upheaval and expansion involving mass migration from Europe to the new world countries, such as the Americas, Canada and Australia. Social issues, such as poor social and living conditions for large numbers of the population and the exclusion of the most vulnerable, were accentuated as the result of rapid industrialisation. Much of the work of social work pioneers, at the time, focussed on issues such as improvements in housing and neighbourhood conditions for poor and migrant groups (settlement houses), and better conditions for prisoners and women's rights (see the Dutch initiative[1]). Early social reformists such as Elizabeth Fry (UK), Arnold Toynbee and Jane Addams[2] (USA), Mary Richmond (UK) and Alice Solomon (Germany), advocated for the provision of services for convicts, migrants, the disadvantaged and displaced groups. They based their interventions on newly emerging sociological, psychological and economic theories that focussed on the social and physical environments of people, the psychological aspects of human beings, and the arrangements of economic and welfare systems. These theories continue to shape social work practice today. Furthermore, most of these pioneers were active in promoting international exchange and strategically fixed their attention to specific structural issues such as child welfare, migration, healthcare and poverty which remain as relevant today as in the past. However, the dimensions and the scale of these problems have clearly changed over the

---

[1] The initiative acknowledges that this compilation is work in progress and provides a space for making suggestions toward including other personalities that were key in shaping social work in particular regions or indeed internationally (historyofsocialwork.org).
[2] Jane Addams first established social work based on research and a structured approach in Chicago, USA.

years as a consequence of the impact of globalisation, climate change and technology on human welfare and development.

The spread of professional social work to other parts of the world is also associated with the power of northern European colonial administrations to govern, control and influence social development in other parts of the world from the 1800s onward. Professional social work played a role in the delivery of social welfare as a form of colonisation and suppression of indigenous peoples and culture by actively exporting particular Christian beliefs into a non-Christian cultural context. The imperialistic ambitions of European countries such as Britain, Spain and France during the 19th and 20th centuries shaped professional social work in the colonised regions of Australia, India, Latin America and Africa. For example, euro-centric ideas and racism often shaped ideas of childhood, childcare and welfare in countries of the global south. The practice of separation of children from indigenous families in Australia and in the USA are prime examples of how such ideologies discriminated against particular types of families (Tamburro, 2013). Even today, racist beliefs appear to underpin the differential and inequitable treatment of minority families and children compared with white families in the USA, and the UK (Roberts, 2002; Statham, 2009). Social work academics (Haug, 2005: 127; Midgley, 1981) have criticised the imperialism of social work, in which a European model of social work has been disseminated around the world and transposed to non-western contexts, ignoring fundamental cultural and power differences and perpetuating an ethos of paternalism.

The internationalisation of the social work profession was further influenced by the social, political and economic conditions in the 1900s and the impact of the two world wars. It was after the atrocities committed during the second world war that the Human Rights Declaration and Convention was established, which provided the impetus for the formation of international organisations such as the International Federation of Social Work (IFSW), the International Association of Social Work (IASW) and the International Council on Social Welfare (ICSW) to promote social work through international platforms (Payne, 2005). These organisations remain important stakeholders in the internationalisation of the profession and in the promotion of norms, standards and approaches for the development of international social work.

Despite the international history of social work, current social work education and practice continues to be shaped by regional and national histories, culture and welfare structures, which then influence professional programs.

Internationalisation of social work today

Nevertheless, given the global scale of social problems and the need to address issues globally, internationalisation within social work education is increasing and the further development of international social work is gaining ground. Social work schools are encouraging student exchanges, links with social work practitioners and schools in other contexts to further promote internationalisation.

However, there is a lack of consensus as to what is meant by internationalisation, both for social work practice and education (Abram and Cruce, 2007; Kendall, 1979). This has often led to an uncritical engagement with the internationalisation of social work and has further muddied the notion of international social work. While student exchange between countries is promoted in social work education, a lack of critical power analysis can lead to a reiteration of dominant power positions rather than promoting change. Examining social work in different contexts can indeed open up alternative ways of thinking and doing. However, uncritical exchanges that do not examine power differences can lead to problematic assumptions that the state of social work practice and provision in one country is superior or inferior to that in other countries (Pawar et al., 2004). For example, students or practitioners involved in international exchange programs can come back from an overseas fieldwork placement with unrealistic views as to the standard of social work or the effectiveness of the welfare system in their country compared to that of other countries (Anand and Das, 2014). It is often common for students to judge the professional standard of social work to be higher in developed countries (e.g. the UK) than in developing countries (e.g. India). It is less frequent that students consider practices to be better in a developing country (e.g. Ghana) as compared to a developed country (e.g. Germany). Neither position represents the views that we are promoting in this book. Simplistic comparative approaches to social work practice across borders and cultures serve to reinforce unequal power relations, paternalistic perspectives and unrealistic beliefs that should be challenged. Moving beyond these comparisons to be critically reflective and reflexive, is what all professionals should aspire to (Anand and Das, 2014).

Finally, we believe that the term international denotes a separation between what exists 'out there' and what exists 'here'. International social work often reinforces positions of local and global, citizen and non-citizen, national and non-national positions which are not only simplistic (Moosa-Mitha, 2014) but dangerous in light of growing nationalism and populism. Furthermore, the term international underplays the complexity of people's lived realities in a globalised world that transcends borders, where such divisions become meaningless or simply obstacles that must be overcome. Furthermore, social work practice in specific countries cannot be understood in isolation from their particular historical, cultural, social and economic contexts.

Opportunities in International Social Work

As argued, though not new, social work and exchange across borders has gained currency in recent times, reflecting the pressures of contemporary global, social, political and economic conditions. For example, the influx of large numbers of asylum seekers into Europe from Middle Eastern countries such as Syria, Iraq, Afghanistan, and Iran between 2014 and 2016 reactivated the consciousness of European social workers and promoted a greater appreciation of the transnational nature of social problems and the scope of practice. Likewise, social work in the post-colonial societies of the global south and in the former Soviet countries is undergoing a process of questioning the cultural appropriateness and relevance of past practices. The context of globalisation demands this engagement as it is increasingly difficult to segregate the national from the international. In everyday practice, social workers increasingly work in agencies, government services and schools where migrants/refugees and children of migrants are clients. In order to appropriately support these clients, recognition of their international and transnational connections is required and the development of services in view of their needs is vital. This not to suggest that international social work is only relevant to migration and cultural issues. Unfortunately, there is a tendency to conceptualise international social work as relating to the problems of so-called 'others', namely other developing countries, other indigenous groups, or other excluded groups. On the contrary, the remit of international social work penetrates all social work practice. The limited engagement by practitioners with international social work is partly explained by a lack of conceptual and ideological clarity in the literature and the concepts used (Lyons et al., 2012; Nagy and Falk, 2000; Powell and Robinson, 2007). While the concept of international social work is extremely valuable to our understanding of the history and development of the profession, it is inherently problematic as it locates social work within national territorial boundaries and presents professional practice in other countries in a comparative framework perpetuating nationalistic frames of thinking (Billig, 1995).

Practitioners have an awareness of the profession's international history, the increasing impact of global issues such as poverty, open conflict, human trafficking and migration in their day-to-day practice. Social workers also find themselves working with international colleagues (Walsh et al., 2010) or delivering new services and interventions adopted from other countries. Social work students who are increasingly travelling across countries and borders for field work education and graduate employment often have exposure to and greater awareness of social work in other countries. Practitioners are justified in asking how relevant theoretical concepts, such as internationalisation and globalisation, are in informing everyday practice. Social Workers require practice models which help them negotiate and sometimes counteract the impact of globalisation in their daily practice. They are often frustrated by the gulf between theory and practice. As academics, our contribution to the profession is to theorise practice, or alternately, operationalise theory into practice models.

The challenge is to engage in a critical manner to support the reordering of unequal power equations. There are many contradictions inherent in our education and practice that make this critical engagement difficult. The confrontation with indigenisation and globalisation that conflict with mainstream ideas and global processes are a sign of these contradictions. Increasing recognition of indigenous knowledge, to widen and diversify the base of social work to also reflect the culture, knowledge, practices and values of people from non-European contexts. Nevertheless, the critical theories and post-colonial theories put forward by Payne (1997) and Bhabha (1994) in terms of the new methods and perspectives offer possibilities (Tamburro, 2013) that need to be recognised by social workers. Post-colonialism studies not only refer to the end of the colonial period but also to the ways in which colonialism continues to occur and the impact of past and ongoing colonialism of people's lives and an understanding of people within this historical continuity. Post-colonial theories and studies also refer to uncovering hidden voices, forgotten histories and resistances. However, these histories and stories cannot be uncovered by mainstream methods that undermine them. The demand for developing new methodologies or decolonising methodologies is thus extremely important to the profession. This can be particularly helpful for social workers as in the main social workers engage with people who are oppressed and whose perspectives are marginalised. An engagement with de-colonial methodologies provides insights not only for working with people in other countries who have experienced colonial histories but also for working within one's own national context by using methods that enable hidden stories to emerge and considering the continuity of people's lives across history and across countries.

Globalisation and International Social Work

As with internationalisation, globalisation is not an entirely new phenomenon and offers both opportunities and challenges for the social work profession. The profession's renewed interest in internationalisation should be considered in terms of not only the highly diverse and contextualised nature of social work, but also the profound impact that global influences and trends have on domestic practice (Dominelli, 2010). The opportunities of globalisation are plentiful and provide possibilities for bringing together people in ways previously undreamt of. This has enabled social issues such as child poverty, elder abuse, human trafficking to be defined and monitored at an international level and combated more strategically at the local level. Arguably, what is problematic, however, is the way in which globalisation enables people, organisations and structures in power to exploit the powerless and to penetrate and erode local culture and traditions. The following section further outlines the globalised context of social work that makes social work's engagement with international social work and global mindedness urgent and extremely relevant.

Globalisation and global problems

The conditions of globalisation have clearly led to a compounding of certain problems at a global level. Thus problems and clients that were previously local and located in particular territories are increasingly global.

The rapid political and economic change that globalisation has brought forward has resulted in more extreme structural inequality within societies and the creation of a 'fourth world', inhabited by people and communities that have lost value either as producers or as consumers in the capitalist and neoliberal economic order (Castells, 1999, 2010). Such groups or communities are often uneducated or functionally illiterate, and/or physically or mentally unable to participate and contribute as equal citizens and are often labelled as vulnerable and needy. This has resulted in a situation where people and places with 'value' are increasingly globally connected and people and places with no, or less, 'value' are disconnected and socially excluded. The poorest people on the planet are most adversely affected through loss of jobs, or low-paid work that is insufficient to provide a decent standard of living, health hazards, rising food and energy prices, environmental degradation, armed conflict and resource depletion (Downey et al., 2010; Freeman, 2004). Disadvantaged and marginalised persons are being forced across national borders in search of security and in attempts to meet their basic human needs. Increasing inequality is a considerable push factor for people to move to different parts of the world for various reasons, i.e. poverty, wars, famine and environmental degradation.

The migration from rural areas to urban areas is a phenomenon that has been occurring globally. While for people with financial means, migration is simple – the process of moving is more challenging for people who do not have resources. Often, such migration is pushed by growing opportunities in cities and lack of sustainable opportunities in rural areas. In many big cities such as, for example, Mumbai, Kolkata and Delhi in India, this migration is posing considerable issues for local people in the cities as well as for the city administration that cannot provide appropriate housing, sanitation and general services for a ballooning population.

This migration is not limited to within geographical nations. People, in search of safety and better livelihoods, are also crossing international boundaries. For example, the city of Kolkata in India sees migration not only from neighbouring rural areas but also from refugee populations from Bangladesh. Similar migration is also seen from Asian and African countries into safer neighbouring countries and even Europe. While migration can be a positive asset for persons moving as well as the receiving countries, it can also prove to be a challenge, in terms of service provision and integration. Clearly, for receiving countries, some of which are hard pressed to prove assistance, migration is perceived as a very difficult topic to deal with. The United Nations (UN) has estimated that 42 million people are seeking refuge globally (most are in Africa). Climate change, resulting in droughts and floods, is anticipated to create further millions of refugees by 2050 (Sanders, 2009). Environmental degradation, capitalistic exploitation and resource scarcity also foster armed conflict leading to further migration of people seeking safety and security. Environmental, financial, demographic and political crises are visible in all countries (Giddens, 2009) and have significant consequences for people and organisational systems.

Other aspects of the globalisation of social problems include the organised drug trade, human trafficking, arms smuggling and terrorism. The drug trade is one of the largest illicit smuggling trades involving huge costs in terms of human lives, crime, loss of livelihoods as well as loss of State revenue. The trade in humans has become the third-highest income earner after arms and drug smuggling (Lyons et al., 2006). This has an impact on social workers, who increasingly work with refugees, with children of migrants in schools and with ethnic communities (often migrant) that are marginalised.

Processes of globalisation have also changed the nature of the welfare state and thereby the conditions of work for many social workers. Austerity measures, cost efficiency and the rationalisation of stretched resources are key neoliberal ideas and result in the withdrawal of the State from economic and welfare spheres. However, the excessive focus on monetary efficiency and performance can undermine the importance of other factors. In addition, this economic efficiency and performance focus can often lead to developments that seek to exploit others for profit. Western neoliberal ideas have resulted in social care and health needs becoming economic spheres of activity open to free market economics (Clarke and Newman, 1997). Managerialism has resulted in privatising of social services (hospitals, care homes, foster care, homes for the elderly) and in an increase in the contract-culture involving competitive tendering of public services. Such changes not only challenge the welfare states commitment to social justice and human rights but in some cases compromise the quality of services and care.

Marginalisation, oppression, vulnerability and exclusion are thus global concerns today. These are structural issues rather than individual problems. To address these problems, social workers must re-examine their strategies and focus more on structural and policy-orientated social work. Without an understanding of the connection between the global and the local, addressing such agendas is simply not possible. Social workers' abilities to understand and connect the local with the global as well as their practical experiences fieldwork place them in a unique position to shape policy in an informed and humane manner. Professionals with such attributes can play a central role in bridging solutions across different levels of praxis.

Globalisation and global solutions

While, globalisation globalises problems and clients, it also globalises opportunities for communication, travel, international employment and exchange. These positive effects benefit sections of people who are able to access global opportunities. For example, the opportunities and possibilities for social workers to travel, explore, work or do internships in other countries is a reflection of how globalisation also eases this mobility.

Technology and communication has profited from globalisation by enabling and providing opportunities for communication, even for marginalised populations. The world today is organised around telecommunication networks with information technologies at the heart of information systems and communication processes. The entire realm of human activity depends on the power of information, as a sequence of technological innovations. Modern communication networks can support quick and local mobilisation of resources in crisis situations. For example, communication and technology plays a significant role even for migrants and refugees as they travel under precarious conditions. These networks were used to support migrants to plan routes, keep in touch and support each other across distances and national boundaries. There is increasing development of technology that intuitively responds to users. For example, it is not uncommon for family members to share experiences, communicate via photos, videos and voice messages instantly across large distances. Technology and robots are increasingly used in the care of people. Social workers need to proactively engage in dialogue and experimentation to see how this technology and communication can be used in service provision to ensure more accessibility and privilege human dignity. However, the difficulty is that in certain cases some people and some localities may not have access to this technology, many do not possess the language skills or may not know how to safely use the technology – thus becoming excluded from these communication networks. This leads to groups of people being silenced. The inappropriate abuse of technology, by cyber predators, criminals and bullies represents new threats to the safety and privacy of people and countries.

Globalisation has also enabled people to come together and take joint and cooperative steps to address many pressing issues, such as environmental damage, climate change, protecting children, joined-up action against perpetrators of trafficking and so on, even when environmental crises are not local. Social workers must play a central role in supporting joint action across borders. This can be done by thinking in global terms, critically linking the local with the global and engaging in a broader dialogue with professionals from elsewhere. This also enables the professional development of social work and to establish the profession on the international level. Social workers must be able and willing to communicate with each other, position themselves and signal their solidarity. While the associations of social workers, such as the International Federation of Social Workers (IFSW) and the International Association of Schools of Social Work (IASSW), are very active, more formats that enable local networking across sites and local–global networking must be developed. These links will no doubt also make visible the obvious links between the local and the global.

The nature and scope of social issues, as in day-to-day social work practice, reflect a convergence of global and local conditions. For sustainable solutions, social workers must consider both local and global aspects and dimensions of their work. Globalisation not only presents similar problems that social workers may have to deal with but it also creates resources and opportunities to work together. Globalisation makes communication and worldwide networks possible through which critical resources such as availability of financial means (such as crowdfunding, donations), sharing expertise, equipment and skills, sharing ideas and timely information can become readily available. Social workers, however, must link the local and the global and imbibe in themselves a sense of the global to actively engage with these developments. Global mindedness can be one approach to enable this.

Global Mindedness as a Bridging Theory

As social work educators and practitioners, the critical negotiation of issues of global power in a local context is increasingly necessary. All problems, irrespective of where they manifest and irrespective of their source, impact all of us directly or indirectly. Global mindedness is presented as a bridging theory that builds on international social work for transformative practice by addressing issues of power across local and global contexts. Bridging theories provide students and practitioners with an understanding of complex relationships, such as the interaction of the global with the local, together with guidance as to how to incorporate a big picture perspective, and at the same time reflect and analyse local concerns, i.e. the capacity to engage in global, local and indigenous issues on an equal footing. Anti-oppressive practice (AOP) is one of the central bridging theories of social work in the UK (Thompson, 2016) and is used extensively to inform our notion of global mindedness.

Potentially useful theories, such as post-modernism, critical theory and indigenous theory, and concepts, such as international social work and transnational social work, tend to be somewhat separated from mainstream social work and are therefore difficult for practitioners and students to apply and see the relevance of. In our opinion, innovative middle-range theories or approaches that bridge the divide between theory and practice are often missing in social work practice. Our concept of global mindedness aims to provide some ideas about how the global and the local could be linked in our practice and teaching. We would like to introduce global mindedness as a way of thinking about and doing social work that seeks to foster dialogue between the local and the global. Reflecting on the history, diversity and the importance of context, together with impact of globalisation, is essential in understanding some of the ways in which powerful global forces interact in local contexts to perpetuate inequalities and oppression among people. An historical analysis of the development of social work helps to critically question the profession's role in reproducing and reinforcing dominant ways of thinking and practice in countries of the global south. In the following chapter, we outline some of the key theories and approaches that shape global mindedness.

Summary

In this first chapter, we have outlined the need for global mindedness. We have highlighted the key debates within international social work highlighting both the possibilities and problems with the concept. Our approach is pragmatic and we realise that globalisation drives the internationalisation of social work. Globalisation also supports contradictory developments. On the one hand, supporting the development of communication and technology and efforts for solidarity, and on the other hand, the processes of globalisation can increase inequality and disadvantage. Thus it is not globalisation, per se, that is good or bad but rather how we use its potential and structure our engagement with it by developing policy frameworks and structures that address and correct inequalities.

We have emphasised that the emerging forces of globalisation mean that individual social workers must develop a greater appreciation of their place within a complex, worldwide system of human activity (Gray et al., 2012. By adopting the term global mindedness in social work, we aim to offer social work practitioners, students and educators an alternative way of thinking about and doing social work practice, education and research which addresses the complex interplay of local social work practice and needs of vulnerable groups with global trends and global pressures that effect our professional understandings. The concept of global mindedness involves an appreciation of diverse ways of working with vulnerable people across the globe guided by a commitment to social justice.

Chapter Questions

- How would/could you define your social work practice and link it with global issues, in terms of:
  - your clients?
  - the problems your clients face?

- What local and international knowledge sources inform your practice?

- How could global and local organisations/agencies support you and your clients?

2 Defining Global Mindedness in Practice: Values, Knowledge and Skills

Introduction

Global mindedness in practice refers to the specific ways of thinking and acting that reflect a critical understanding of the global dimensions of localised oppression, injustice, marginalisation and social exclusion. The knowledge, values and skills upon which it is based involve concepts familiar to most social workers, namely power and social change, human rights underpinned by humanitarian values, as well as professional practice. These concepts will be discussed in more detail in this chapter. The concepts of globalisation, localisation and power are central to developing global mindedness. The influence of globalisation has meant that the scope of social work extends well beyond the nation-welfare state. The operationalisation of global mindedness involves the recognition of the intersectionality of social issues and the reworking of social work values, perspectives, theories and interventions that can be applied across local and global levels.

The aim of global mindedness in practice is not to create another vision of international social work. Nor is the intent to compare and contrast different social work traditions. While thought provoking, comparisons introduce an unjust and incomplete understanding which is often biased in its treatment of other traditions of social work practice. Rather, the aim is to facilitate discourse and critical debate by acknowledging and exploring competing and interacting perspectives, within and across social, cultural and geographical contexts (Payne, 1997). Through the concept of global mindedness, this book aims to engage with how human rights and anti-oppression practice can be exercised at the point of interaction between the local and the global. Using case examples, the book attempts to address the moral and cultural challenges encountered in this process by deconstructing and reconstructing knowledge and our understanding of these challenges.

What Is Global Mindedness?

The term global mindedness has been considered in the field of education, and in the context of global citizenship. For example, Andreotti et al. (2015) discuss global mindedness in the context of student exchange. They refer to global mindedness in terms of being open minded; seeing the big picture; being open to new things; seeing differences as richness; having awareness of one's own prejudices; and having a willingness to interact with different people. Global mindedness from a social work context, however, involves a critical exploration of rights, differences, social and cultural boundaries and occupational spaces. Global mindedness (Andreotti et al., 2015) as applied to international social work may be described as:

- an analysis of social issues from both local and global perspectives;
- an ability and commitment to uncover hidden power dynamics;
- an awareness of mobility, flexibility and the shifting or pushing out of boundaries, borders and time;
- an openness to explore new ideas and perspectives and engage with people from diverse backgrounds;
- a pursuit of connectivity and solidarity for the purpose of achieving social change.

Building Global Mindedness

The central themes that frame the concept of global mindedness involve the consideration of local–global–local perspectives, power and anti-oppressive practice and human rights. Figure 2.1 illustrates the relationship between the three concepts and global mindedness.

Local–global–local (L–G–L) perspectives

Global mindedness requires students, practitioners and academics to understand and engage with the complex relationship between the local and the global (Gray, 2005; Gray and Fook, 2004; Ife, 2001). In the context of social work practice, *local* refers to the direct communication between people, clients and workers. *Global*, on the other hand, refers to the interaction between individuals, systems and actors that may not be directly linked but are related to each other through structures, networks, processes and mechanisms that have an impact on each other. Neither concept is restricted to spatial structures (levels, space, scales, distances etc.) (Guy, 2009) and both may include temporal experiences as well. The term *glocal* has become popular and is useful to describe the coexistence

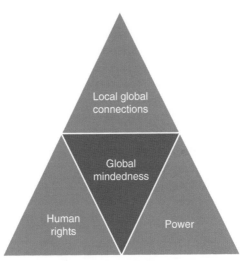

Figure 2.1: Central Themes in Global Mindedness

of global influences in day-to-day local experiences (Livholts and Bryant, 2017). The relationship between the global and the local may be mutual and co-dependent, but in many cases is beset with conflict and contra-dictions. Global minded social workers must negotiate these tensions in daily practice. For example, in 2017 in Essen, Germany (Deutsche Welle, 2018), charities had to rethink their strategy of distributing food to the needy due to increasingly high demand that could not be met. This rise in demand was partly due to increasing migration in Germany that put a strain on local charities as well as putting local need in competition with the needs of migrants. This case highlights the classic tensions between the global and the local. Globalisation has increasingly driven migration, as argued in the previous chapter. However, the interaction between global migration and local needs, practices and demands often leads to conflict and scarcity. This has also been the reason that in most countries there is an increasing resistance to non-national migration. For global minded social workers, the issue is to appropriately meet the needs of all persons irrespective of nationality or location. Global minded social workers must attempt to meet the needs of all persons by working across different levels. Social workers need to address the issues of meeting needs by working at the level of administrative and financial policy and ensur-ing systems are in place to offer support to those that need it, and also to consider the reasons that drive need-based migration and attempt to address it at source. Practitioners also need to work locally to ensure that solutions are found that are inclusionary.

At one level, the aim is to protect the local needs of clients and prac-tices from the penetration of the global influences. At another level, it is essential to understand and work with global influences to resolve issues, enable connectivity and solidarity and ensure sustainability. Global minded social workers constantly analyse and link local problems with global issues, modify ideas and influences, and adapt new knowledge and understanding to inform their practice.

Global mindedness in practice involves an understanding of how domestic social work, and its particular histories within social policy, legislative, national contexts, is shaped by global events, relationships and movements. Concerns as to the homogenisation or Mcdonaldisation (managerial application of efficiency, calculability, predictability, standardisation and control of social work practice and the treatment of clients as consumers) of the international social work movement are legitimate (Dustin, 2007). However, it must also be acknowledged that local practices may inform global practices and agendas. There are examples of local practices that have been developed within particular communities and cultural contexts becoming internationally recognised methods of practice in social work. Yet a common praxis mistake is to become entrenched in the local context of our practice, ignoring the causal impact of global factors on our day-to-day work. Alternatively, we sometimes become so oblivious to the power and predominance of global trends and influences that we fail to question their impact on local communities and environment. However, the intention is not to privilege local or international perspectives on practices, as this is the antithesis of our aims, but to open dialogue and develop new insights and critical learning as to how the global and local shape our practice.

The ability to understand the local and global connection is perhaps the most critical stage in this process, and is simplified in Figure 2.2.

This process of linking the global with the local, starts and ends at the level of the local, as this is the point of direct contact. It is essential to understand that the local and the global are merely the spaces where we have direct or indirect connection.

Human rights

Being a global minded social worker is to enable an unwavering commitment to social justice and human rights for all. Human rights are considered universal; belonging to everybody regardless of race, nation, culture, sex, age, ability, beliefs or behaviour. Human rights are indivisible; and inseparable, and belong together as a package. They are inalienable and should not be denied for an individual or a group. *First generation human rights* refer to individual and personal rights such as freedom of speech, freedom of assembly, justice before the law, freedom of religion, political participation, and freedom from discrimination. Economic, social and cultural rights, such as the right to education,

Figure 2.2: Local–Global–Local Connections

health, employment, housing, income, security, choice of marriage partner, and cultural expression, are referred to as *second generation human rights*. Human rights are often used as a measure of equity and diversity internationally. While collective rights refer to environmental rights, the right to benefit from economic development, the right to community cohesion and harmony are considered as the *third generation human rights*.

It has been argued, previously, that the human rights approach is not without its tensions and contradictions. Human rights are based on a western construction of rights, i.e. secularised, gendered and based on utilitarianism (Ife, 2007). Furthermore, guarantees of human rights are provided by the nation state and this challenges and often undermines the 'universality' of human rights. Nevertheless, 'human rights for all' is and remains an ideal vision for social workers. Social workers are essentially engaged to develop structures that enable the translation of human rights as lived experiences. To realise this aim, transformative changes that involve creative as well as collective processes are necessary. For example, music, art, theatre, poetry, dance, love, laughter, games and the experience of nature can be conveyors of new 'knowledge' and create possibilities for creative enterprises. Likewise, social change and a commitment to human rights necessarily involve collective action through advocacy, resistance, community work and social development. Economic and social rights are not so much a claim made by an individual, but a process toward creation of structures for human communities (Parel, 1997).

Human rights are constructed, understood and experienced collectively. For example, the realisation of one's rights is possible only through the realisation of the rights of others. This collective ownership and experience of human rights locates a common humanity at the core of social work activity and carries a vision of a 'better world'. Embedded in this vision is the idea and purpose of global mindedness.

Power

The central tenet that makes social work a global profession is its commitment to addressing oppression by working in collaboration with people and communities. An understanding of power, its dynamics and the mechanisms through which power can lead to discrimination and oppression are key themes and ideas that guide social work practice and determine the interventions for practice. Globalisation in contemporary power structures, as explored in the previous chapter, privileges the 'haves' and marginalises the 'have nots'. Furthermore, as explored in the concepts of the internationalisation of social work, established power structures often value European perspectives and reiterate colonial ways of understanding. The understanding of power, privilege and oppression is vital in global mindedness. Global minded social workers must use critical theories and interventions to navigate local–global tensions. Issues of power, not only the lack thereof but also privilege, must be considered from a local and case by case perspective as well as from a global and structural perspective. It is this engagement with power that makes social work a critical profession. Social work often focusses on communities that are oppressed and lack power. The processes by which groups and communities that are privileged and have power continue to maintain structures, and the processes that help them sustain these positions, is seldom a theme in social work. Nevertheless, dismantling these mechanisms at local and global levels is vital for social justice if an equal society is to be made attainable.

Power is an awkward and slippery concept (Smith, 2008), but central to understanding how global forces influence and shape local conditions and the potential of people to resist global trends. Power is exerted or enforced by means of dominant ideas, privileges and structures

(Smith, 2008) and is used for both positive and negative purposes. However, the globalisation of power tends to privilege groups of people and to generate multiple forms of oppression which intersect, for example, racism, sectarianism, sexism, ageism, disablism and more extreme examples of social and health inequality (Dominelli and Campling, 2002). Anti-oppressive practice in social work is premised on a critical analysis of how privilege and dominance is exercised and reproduced (Pease, 2010).

Global mindedness involves asking critical questions in relation to power; for example, who is oppressed, in what respects are they oppressed, who holds the power, how is power exercised, how is discrimination or oppression maintained and how can power imbalances and injustice be addressed (Smith, 2008). For example, a global minded social worker working with refugee groups should understand the interconnections between the positions of those seeking refuge, the reasons for the requirement for refuge, as well as the implications of refuge seeking at the international, national and local levels. Global mindedness urges social workers to dig deeper and unearth global interconnectivity that render people vulnerable and powerless.

Any reference to anti-oppressive practice and global mindedness must involve an acknowledgement of the power possessed by social work clients. Professional social work practice is shaped by the rules and regulations of the employing agency or institution (Healy, 2014). Social workers hold power in terms of knowledge and ideas, occupy positions of power and are supported by legislative frameworks that help to empower them. Individual social workers also hold power inherent to their class, sex, ability, race, nationality, access, language, culture and other factors.

Both anti-oppressive practice and global mindedness require an examination of one's own sense of power or powerlessness, as the case may be. While it may not be possible for all social worker practitioners or students to engage in radical activism to change power structures, it is possible to seek opportunities to organise and collectively respond to social issues. Interventions such as empowerment, advocacy, lobbying and other skills in anti-oppressive practice are effective processes in bringing about change. Professional education provides social work students with knowledge of how to operationalise their roles as agents of change either within or outside social organisations and systems.

Working beyond individual levels of practice presents ongoing challenges but it is possible for practitioners to extend their power base by networking with other disciplines such as allied and social professions and by developing joint alliances. These allies can be representatives of civil society such as community advocacy groups, which may be in a strategic position to undertake political and social action on behalf of clients. Collective, collaborative and creative methods of operationalising our commitment to social justice are to be encouraged in social work education, practice and research. Global mindedness in practice not only involves the critical analysis of power and privilege but the exercising of power, across different levels of practice.

While a global–local perspective, human rights and power are the main themes, global mindedness is underpinned by specific values, knowledge and skills that are outlined in the following section.

Values, Knowledge and Skills for Global Mindedness

Certain values, knowledge and skills are key in developing global minded-ness as they provide insights as to how local and global influences interact to create or challenge social injustice (Figure 2.3).

Values

Having respect for local practices and, at the same time being open to global influences, is guided by a commitment to humanitarian values. Values inform ethics and ethical standards, which are crucial in deter-mining professional relationship with clients and to social work at large (Reamer, 2013). Social work values are codified in professional ethics and a quick review of social work codes of ethics across the globe highlights the level of diversity (Banks, 2012). However, by virtue of its diverse and complex nature, the practice of social work is fraught with ethical dilemmas. Core values in social work, such as compassion, autonomy, non-judgement, social justice and fairness reflect dominant western, Judeo-Christian constructions, with primacy given to the individual

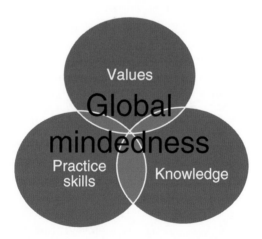

Figure 2.3: Values, Knowledge and Skills for Global Mindedness

and to liberal democratic contexts rather than the collective societies (Ife, 2001). While it is important to question the universality of social work values, it is just as important to believe that we have something in common with other human beings (Ife, 2001). There is no easy solution to this issue of universality versus relativity, other than continual dialogue as to what is important for people (Donnelly, 1999). The recent introduction of the Global Social Work Statement of Ethical Principles (2018) will no doubt contribute to this debate.

The need to see ourselves as connected with a global community is also important to enable and recognise the humanities of others and refer to 'us'. We must overcome the 'them' and 'us' dichotomy. While our political lives are still embedded in national states, in economic and social spheres, our engagement extends across national boundaries. The idea of being connected globally remains a powerful counter argument against increasing nationalism and highlights the ways in which people and places have always been connected, dependent and have shared destinies. Feeling globally connected involves an understanding of the world as one unified system and a responsibility to view the interests of individual nations with the overall needs of the planet. This idea is useful in promoting global mindedness as it reinforces ongoing engagement with new political, social, environmental and alternative worldviews beyond nationalistic interests and concerns.

Knowledge

The use of theory in social work is highly contestable and debatable (Gray and Webb, 2012). Social work has been influenced by different histories and theoretical traditions as well as different disciplines. For example, psychological and systems theories have been influential in shaping social work in the USA, while in Germany theories of social pedagogy are fundamental to social work education. In the UK and Australia, sociological and psychological theories have been instrumental in shaping practice, while in Finland social policy has provided the knowledge base for the profession. Global mindedness requires a critical perspective and an understanding of these traditions of knowledge and provides new opportunities for theory creation, development and testing. This involves a greater awareness of the broadening and dynamic influence of different reference sources or disciplines on social work. Different sources of knowledge are thus relevant and necessary for global mindedness and critical engagement with issues of power.

Scientific knowledge: Social work claims to be a profession based on scientific theories and understanding of the world. Social work knowledge and theory have been informed by various disciplines such as psychology, education, sociology, social policy and other social sciences. Social work is also increasingly influenced by theories of management and economics. Thus, social workers draw from a wide and eclectic knowledge base to inform their practice. In many countries, social workers are required to base their interventions on evidence and scientific methods. For example, in Finland, reference is made to the concept of *scientific social work*, while in the UK, the concept of evidence-informed or evidence-based social work is promoted. There is increasingly a call to improve transparency, and measure the outcomes and effectiveness of social work interventions under the auspices of accountability. Social workers are also required to reflect, justify and theorise their understanding of problems and solutions.

However, the privileging of positivist approaches have tended to reinforce colonialist ends by encouraging practitioners to ignore inherent biases, and to adopt evidence-based practice that may be blind to cultural difference and alternative sources of knowledge (Ife, 2001). Evidence is neither neutral nor value-free and global minded social workers need to critically examine evidence and use it to inform rather than base their practice on it by using a local–global–local framework. An appreciation of cultural sensitivity and reflection upon one's own values are essential skills in this process. Social work practitioners are aware their work with clients is not a measurable scientific 'intervention'. Non-empirical knowledge is characteristically local, grounded and specific to a particular place, culture or group. This knowledge represents the local dimensions that should inform global debates. Social workers operate under local conditions and it is local knowledge that is necessary in order to understand the people whom they work with, their problems, their needs and their aspirations.

***Indigenous knowledge*:** The importance of post-colonial theory in providing a critical framework from which to examine the history of local and global traditions in social work was previously discussed. Indigenous knowledge offers a unique insight as to local–global tensions and the risks of imposing international ideas onto local communities. Indigenous knowledge is premised on the understanding that there are different ways of being (ontology), knowing (epistemology), and doing (methodology) and questions the morality of colonial imposition (Martin and Mirraboopa, 2003). Indigenous theory has been introduced into Australian social work ethics and education to prepare students for working with Aboriginal communities (Green and Baldry, 2008). This approach can be applied more generally when working with difference. It involves approaching social work from a position of not knowing and seeking to learn about the client's experiences and thoughts.

A major criticism of indigenous social work is that it can result in an extreme form of cultural relativism and the acceptance of abusive behaviours which could violate basic human rights (Ife, 2008). To what extent indigenous social work theory will be integrated into mainstream practice around the world is yet unclear. However, the approach is useful for fostering an appreciation of difference and diversity that is central to our notion of global mindedness.

Analysing different sources of knowledge and information is key to addressing power. Social work practice is not only based on scientific evidence, but also on what we as humans value and prioritise. This involves re-evaluating, reframing and reworking knowledge, based on the historical continuities of peoples' lives. Social work practice removed from people's contexts and based purely on scientific methods is at risk of not being critical and anti-oppressive. The main task of social workers is to address oppression in a globalising world. However, the increasing complexity of knowledge and information sources makes it difficult to tease out the dimensions of power across different levels of the local and the global. Global mindedness presents one possibility as to how social workers can rise to this challenge.

Practice skills for global mindedness

Social work is an applied academic profession. The uniqueness of social work is that it not only develops theories to understand issues and analyse problems but also to apply them in practice, referred to as praxis. Actively working with vulnerable people requires an ability to simultaneously manage different perspectives, working at different levels, engaging with emotions and feelings, dealing with crises and developing strategies to effectively communicate with people working toward empowerment.

Since social workers engage with people from diverse backgrounds (not only race and ethnicity but also poverty, disability, gender, old age, sexual identity), the challenge is to apply knowledge and address issues of oppression without oppressing people and their way of life. All people are products of their cultures and hence working with people requires competently working with people in their life worlds. This ability to understand issues and work with people in their cultural contexts is cultural competence. While cultural competence is necessary and applicable in all cases, dealing with groups that belong to the same cultural milieus as that of the social worker may seem easier. The notion of cultural competence thus often takes the dominant culture as a given and the concept is often applied to in reference with minority groups or 'other' cultures. Thus contemporary social work education has a tendency to reduce the understanding of cultural competence to a series of do's and don'ts for practitioners, based on stereotypical pieces of information (Betancourt et al., 2005; Kumagai and Lypson, 2009). This results in an oversimplification of the concept of culture and encourages the use of broad generalisations and stereotyping (Ben-Ari and Strier, 2010; Chau et al., 2011 Furlong and Wight, 2011; Harrison and Turner, 2011). In this way, cultural competence is used to further minoritise groups by focussing on difference, ignoring culture as a dynamic concept and limiting analysis of systems of discrimination.

However, we argue that critical cultural competence is necessary for all social work and recognition of the culture of a client is central to all work with individuals, groups and communities. Critical cultural competence encompasses a set of skills that enables social workers to:

- understand the nuances and complexity of a group of people, their history and belief systems;
- use skills that allow people and communities to voice their needs;
- develop strategies of intervention that respect people's environments, ways of life and philosophies;
- reflect on their own actions and be willing to transform and change in the process.

Cultural competence should seek to support people's ways of perceiving the world through a critical examination of power (critical), privilege (reflexivity), self-awareness (reflection) and a commitment to change (transformative practice) (Das and Anand, 2016).

To effectively engage in anti-oppressive practice, social workers need to be constantly self-reflective and reflexive in their work. Reflection refers to the constant engagement with one's own emotions, values, judgements and feelings so that the social worker does not impose one's own ideas onto others. A lack of reflection can lead to the overemphasis of one's own perspectives or biases instead of imagining creative ways of compromise and working with the client. Nationalistic attitudes are embedded in our everyday lives in an intricate way, and making the connection with the global requires constant questioning and reworking.

The reflexivity of social workers is important for social workers' engagement with people and communities. Reflexivity incorporates understanding the impact of the social worker's role and intervention from the clients' perspectives. In the process of empowerment, a social worker is a key actor who also undergoes a process of change. This change is as much part of the empowerment for the social worker as it is for the clients. This form of engagement incorporates the 'we' and diminishes the 'other'. Social workers work *with* people. For examples, social workers are often criticised for offering services in a paternalistic manner rather than seeking to develop client-directed services. Reflexivity leads to further personal reflection.

Critical self-reflection and reflexivity together enable greater analysis of positions of power to counter inequalities, particularly in the case of working with vulnerable people. It enables practitioners to understand client resistance and ambivalence in response to power being exercised. For example, the practice of a social worker born and raised in a particular neighbourhood in London will differ vastly if they work in another town in the UK, in another European country, in the USA or in China. Reflexivity enables a social worker to examine their own positionality and how that impacts on the power relations with the people they engage with.

Global minded social workers also need to be able to use their skills to enable work across different levels of practice work and to effectively incorporate cultural competency across these levels. Working with individuals requires different cultural ways of looking at the individual in relation to his or her family and the community or State. For example, social work practice in some western societies fosters client self-determination and the rights of the individual, values which are reflected in their national codes of social work ethics. However, social work practice in other European countries privileges the reciprocal relationship between the individual and the State and their practice approaches attempt to promote citizenship using ideas from social pedagogy. Working with individuals incorporates many psycho-social principles that currently dominate practice in the 'developed' world (Jordan, 1978, 2001; Payne, 2005). However, working with individuals in societies where social relations are more extended and the individual's identity is more closely linked to their group relations, often involves additional elements of working with familial contexts and using a systems framework. Working with groups is underpinned by different theories and skills that can provide a different orientation to 'social change' in social work. The problems that clients face are complex and often so entrenched that it can be counter-productive to just intervene at an individual level. Working at the level of the group is a highly effective method of enabling groups of people with similar problems or groups of people who are equally affected by a similar problems to work together. Thus group work can effectively be used within family contexts as well as with persons who share a similar problem or concern. Group work is common for women facing domestic violence, persons dependent on substances, persons with intellectual disabilities, supporting self-help groups, developing educational programs, parent–teacher groups and so on. Working at the level of the community can involve different ways of engaging with communities, developing projects for and/or with community groups. It is clear that individuals, groups and communities are also globally inter-linked through diasporic and social networks. Thus local issues are often played out in international contexts through these networks. This is another area where the global–local connections become very apparent.

Finally, another area of intervention for social workers is at the level of social policy aimed at provision of services, equal distribution and access of resources across a population. Social policy also pays particular attention to marginalised groups of people such as women, children, young people, people with disabilities, people with mental health conditions and so on (Cheyne et al., 2005). While most social workers study social policy as part of their professional education they do not necessarily see themselves as policy makers or influential in the development of policy. However, development of good social policy necessarily depends on the solid understanding of the needs of people on the ground as well as availability of thorough data and research to inform decision-making. Furthermore, as social workers understand the causes and consequences of communities of marginalised people, they can play an important and critical role in supporting the development of social policy that breaks these cycles of marginalisation and addresses structural issues.

Global minded social work, practitioners need to be able to deal with the complexities of the global–local connections without losing connection with the people they are working with.

Global Mindedness in Practice: Structure of the Following Chapters

Historically, social work practice has been shaped and defined by the services and organisations that employ professionals. For example, child protection involves individual casework with families and structural social work involves policy reform. Yet the reality is that social workers frequently intervene with and move between working with individuals of all ages, families and communities, simultaneously. Domestic practice is multidimensional, at different levels of the micro, mezzo and macro. Artificial categories of clients are defined by agencies or services employing social workers and not the profession. This often creates a mind-set where services are provided only within these categories. In fact, most social work practice necessarily involves intergenerational work, and in most examples of social work practice services can be (and should be) delivered across micro, mezzo and macro levels. Research data and data gathered from services and service users become useful and important when we are able to map these services across levels. This enables us to view needs from different perspectives and offer joined-up creative solutions. For example, child protection work practitioners primarily working with adult parents and in the case of gerontological social work practitioners frequently working with older adults. Both fields of practice involve interventions with individual clients, families and services within policy frameworks. Furthermore, across both types of cases social workers can operate at a micro level, i.e. at the level of the family, or at a mezzo level, i.e. at the level of the group or community, or at the level of policy to create sustainable structures that support the positive development of vulnerable groups.

To enable a broader understanding of working with diverse client groups and across different intervention levels, this book attempts an alternative categorisation to present examples of global mindedness in practice. The concept of global mindedness is explored using case studies across four chapters that consider: protection work, diversity work, structural work and sustainability work. We would point out, however, that these four categories are not exhaustive in any way and work in each of these areas overlaps with other areas. For example, practitioners are involved in advocating for changes to social policy, promoting diversity, aiming for Sustainability as well as undertaking protection intervention in a single child abuse case. The categories of practice outlined seek to include both traditional roles of social work as well as more emerging roles within structural work and sustainability work.

Each of the proceeding four chapters provides an outline of the nature of the work together with an outline of four international case examples, chosen to demonstrate global mindedness in practice. Each case study will be analysed using a process of critical reflection; firstly describing and identifying the issues, secondly by giving a critical analysis of the context and factors involved and finally reworking an understanding relevant for local practice. At the end of each case study, reflective questions addressing the values, knowledge and practice skills for global mindedness are posed. These questions are meant to provoke further thought in terms of how the local and the global connect in everyday practice. Through engagement with these questions, we would like readers to experience the relevance and possibilities for global mindedness in their own practice. Furthermore, we hope this will be a resource for educators teaching international social work and enable problem-based learning that can be applied to local and global contexts. Examples are drawn from various levels of practice, i.e. individual, group work, community and nation work, as well as in terms of the different functions that social workers can undertake. The examples are juxta-positioned across different countries highlighting differences and similarities but more importantly helping to develop a complex understanding of issues rather than simplistic comparisons that can re-assert unequal power relations. The aim is to facilitate discourse and critical debate exploring competing and interacting perspectives.

Summary

Global mindedness is informed by an understanding of local–global–local dynamics, power and human rights. It is operationalised by values, knowledge and skills which underpin these concepts. Furthermore, global mindedness encourages a pushing of boundaries and imagining social work beyond nationalistic confines, social work roles that incorporate the development of policy, law and legislation that reflects contemporary lives and provides vulnerable persons a voice in society. Global mindedness also involves a futuristic orientation and the ability to anticipate the needs of people and trajectories of social phenomena. The global context also presents challenges and opportunities and global minded social workers need to be able to work critically and creatively to identify problems, issues and power nexus's but also to creatively use available resources to suggest, strive for and enable change.

In summary being global minded involves:

- a commitment to advocate for the rights of all;
- an ability to define and fight for human rights and justice as a global citizen;
- a commitment to critical self-reflection and reflexivity;
- engaging with and embracing diversity;
- understanding and applying critical cultural competence;
- an ability to uncover underlying assumptions and see relationships of power and dominance locally and globally;
- pushing boundaries by challenging nationalistic frames of practice that exclude vulnerable people;
- building solidarity between peoples

However, being global minded does *not* mean:

- ignoring local or indigenous practices or issues;
- ignoring histories and identities of people;
- prioritising international or national mandates and ignoring local concerns;
- categorising people into simplistic categories by language, gender, sexuality, ethnicity, race, nationality, religion etc.;
- creating boundaries, engaging in unfair comparisons or only viewing social work practices in other contexts in superficial and descriptive ways.

Chapter Questions

- Identify examples in your local practice where international issues have become apparent (e.g. forced migration, trafficking, climate change, technology, diversity, right-wing politics, poverty).

- Consider how borders of professional practice have been challenged and identify the consequences for social work intervention.

- What human rights' dilemmas do you face in your practice and how do you address them?

3 Global Mindedness in Protection Work

Introduction

The protection of vulnerable groups in society is of concern to most governments and represents the basis of national and international social and welfare policy legislation. Protection work covers different activities and populations, i.e. general adult safeguarding, child protection and welfare, work preventing elder abuse and working with persons experiencing domestic violence. A common feature of protection work is the assessment and provision of services and interventions to people who are in some way vulnerable or at risk of harm at different stages of their life course, i.e. childhood, adulthood and older age. However, this function is not restricted to protective responsibilities but may include prevention of risk, rescue from abuse or neglect and counselling, as well as developing safeguarding protocol and policies. Internationally, protection work represents a core function in child welfare, drug and alcohol and mental health. It could be argued that protection work increasingly defines and dominates professional social work.

What Is Protection Work?

Social workers assist some of the most vulnerable groups of people in our society who are at risk of harm because they either lack the capacity to make informed decisions, or face adverse social and/or health issues, or may be exposed to various forms of exploitation or abuse. Protection work is characterised by having to negotiate the rights of different clients, which may conflict with each other, and manage the tensions between client efficacy, self-determination and protection. In protecting the rights of children and adults, social workers are guided by a legislative and moral framework mandated by the State and society. By its very nature, protection work often involves contradictory elements such as offering care and compassion on one hand and using threat of control and punitive legal action on the other hand. For example, people suffering from mental health conditions, who are considered to be at risk to themselves or others, may be legally sectioned and held against their will in institutional care. The role of health and social care professionals is to provide for their clients' needs while respecting their wishes. However, social workers in protection work have to deal with conflicts when the assessed needs of their clients are not congruent with their wishes or the wishes of their families. In some instances, the protection role may extend to political advocacy and prevention work, depending on the availably of resources and the understanding of the scope of protection work.

The type and extent of protection work undertaken by social workers is determined by the welfare system, policies and legislation of the country concerned. For example, Devaney and McGregor (2017) identify different types of child welfare systems in terms of their orientation toward risk management, provision of welfare and how they meet community needs. They describe systems in Australia, the USA and the UK as being focussed on protective risk management, with Nordic and central European countries being more welfare orientated.

The use of the term protection work in this chapter is a deliberate attempt to avoid the separation of adult and child protection work. In the UK, for example, the division between adult social care and child protection is reinforced in social work education by the teaching of the two as distinct fields of practice. Protection work, whether with children, youth or adults, involves common elements such as an understanding of human rights and the assessment of need and risk. This is not to suggest that adults are to be treated like children or that children should be treated like adults. It is clear that young people and adults differ in their capacity for decision making. Adults, who have capacity to make decisions, should be afforded self-determination and autonomy, even if they choose to make seemingly poor decisions. In most cases, children under a certain age are not legally considered to have decision-making capacity. However, this age varies considerably between countries and may reflect different social and cultural views of the status of the child and their development. Parents, guardians or representatives of the State make decisions on the behalf of children, often based on rather vague notions of 'welfare' and 'best interest'. In some cases, it could be argued that such practices may ignore the rights of the child under the UN Convention on the Rights of the Child. Likewise, the rights and voice of adults with mental health or learning disabilities, and older people, are frequently ignored in legal and welfare practices and contravene international conventions and rights. Therefore, an important role of social workers is to advocate for the rights of the individual in the context of protection work.

Protection work at an individual level also involves assessments of the client's needs and wishes which are then translated into a care plan which is managed by a social worker or allied health professional. Case management, as a way of working at the individual level, is one of the key social work approaches in protection work worldwide. Care plans may be formulated to include supportive measures for individuals and families. In more extreme cases, legal measures that require more formal interventions, that may be contrary to the wishes of clients and their families, may be necessary. Case management also involves the coordination and integration of service elements from different administrative units and service providers. Since, protection work can involve measures that go against the norms and wishes of the clients, there is often high ambivalence and resistance from clients. This makes this work challenging and requires a thorough examination of rights and needs of the clients.

The following diagram reflects the ongoing requirement to balance care and control aspects in protection work by appropriately considering the needs and wants of clients (Figure 3.1).

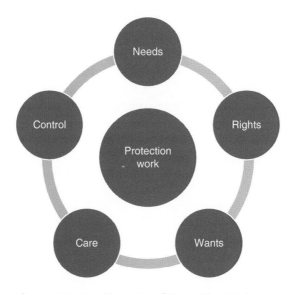

Figure 3.1: Key Elements of Protection Work

While protection work finds expression in social work services around the world, notions of vulnerability and risk differ between different cultures. We explore these issues further in the next section.

Understanding Vulnerability, Risk and Agency

Some questions that are central to an examination of protection work from a global mindedness perspective include:

- Who protects?
- What groups of people are recognised as needing protection?
- Why is protection deemed necessary and in what situations?
- How is individual agency and choice respected in decision making?
- What are the desired outcomes of protection work?

The above questions attempt to tease out the assumptions that underlie the nature of protection work in any given social or cultural context. The legal and administrative framework for the delivery of protection is shaped by the social, economic and historical context of each country or region and reflect the socio-economic and cultural norms of a particular culture or context. For example, in the socio-economic context of the UK, the welfare system strives to protect children from poverty, neglect, abuse and/or other factors which may place the development of the child at risk. However, in developing countries, poverty is conceptualised as a risk to the family and the child is part of the family. Another example is the use of corporal punishment by parents. In the UK, corporal punishment of children is considered as physical abuse and would warrant action by social workers. In many other cultures, corporal punishment is often seen as a disciplinary tool, rather than an protection issue. The debate over the use of corporal punishment has become political, even though up until recently corporal punishment was the universal norm. Likewise, notions of 'what' persons need to be protected from can change historically. In the 19th century, for example, the age of sexual consent ranged between 10 and 14 years (Waites, 2005). Children of these ages would be considered minors today and sexual acts toward children of this age would be illegal and morally not acceptable.

We consider a more contemporary case of elder abuse to explore issues around who needs to be protected and from what. We explore elder abuse in the context of Northern Ireland (UK) and the Republic of Ireland (RoI) to highlight how perspectives differ and how a global minded view can support a more integrated view of key issues. In the case of abuse of older people, social policy and practice vary significantly across national borders (WHO, 2002; Penhale et al., 1995) reflecting cultural, social and economic norms. In the USA a complex system of elder law has been developed across the different states to protect older people from being physically, economically or psychologically abused. In comparison, the UK national policy is based on the concept of *vulnerable adult* and has in place a system of adult protection. The following case example explores the importance of local definitions in understanding the global phenomena of elder abuse.

Example 3.1

Local and International Definitions and Responses to Elder Abuse (RoI, UK)

Identifying the issues: In the Republic of Ireland, the concept of elder abuse forms the basis of specialist services to support older people in local communities. The Northern Ireland (NI) model of service provision is not specifically age related and places emphasis on vulnerability, risk and protection (Taylor, 2006; Taylor and Donnelly, 2006). It relies on reporting and investigation protocols, and the monitoring of professional practice (Killick and Taylor, 2009). The RoI approach is focussed on older people over the age of 65 years, with an emphasis on the assessment of individual need, and the provision of existing support services delivered through a system of specialist workers.

Different responses to elder abuse between the two jurisdictions can be explained in terms of Harbison's model (Harbison and Morrow, 1998) with NI programs favouring a protectionist approach and the RoI policy leaning toward a paternalistic orientation. Both approaches conceptualise elder abuse as being located in individual and familial pathology. They both involve the need to eliminate risk, control the behaviour of the perpetrator and care for the vulnerable older person. However, research (Lafferty et al., 2012) indicates that many older people experience some form of abuse at some stage in their lives and that ageism is endemic to western societies and is increasingly becoming so in countries of the global south.

Critical analysis: The paucity of research on older people's views and experience of abuse further reduces opportunities for older people to inform social policy. Irish research studies have tended to focus on professional practice (Cooper et al., 2009; Daly and Coffey, 2010; Killick and Taylor, 2012) or the general public's perceptions of elder abuse (Hussein et al., 2007). A RoI report on Older Peoples Experiences of Mistreatment and Abuse (2012) and the World Health Organization's Missing Voices (2002) report have recognised that the restrictive definition of elder abuse is problematic. These studies conclude that older people are more concerned about neglect, isolation, abandonment and social exclusion, denial of human, legal and medical rights, deprivation of choices and decisions, status, finances and respect, than physical manifestations of abuse. Other studies have also indicated how policies and practices tend to reinforce negative stereotypes of vulnerability of older people and contribute to the older person's growing fear of losing agency, self-determination and basic human rights (van Bavel et al., 2010; Dow and Joosten, 2012). Data from the RoI study conducted by the National Centre for the Protection of Older People (2012) indicated that participants tended to experience more than one type of abuse and in some instances by more than one abuser. These studies reinforce the conceptualisation of elder abuse as a form of ageism involving the denial of social rights, as opposed to notions of vulnerability and the need for increased protection strategies that address the problem at the societal level rather than only at the individual level (Bowes and Daniel, 2010; Phelan, 2008; Peri et al., 2009; WHO, 2011). The persistent 'othering' of older people not only makes it easier for older people to be maltreated and exploited at a societal level but has a damaging impact on the self-identity and personhood of older people (Dow and Joosten, 2012; Kitwood, 1996; Whitbourne and Sneed, 2002). Combating social isolation, promoting social connection and intergenerational relations, treating older people with respect and dignity, and educating the general public around positive attitudes toward older people should be the basis for preventive and sustainable strategies for promoting older people's social rights (WHO, 2011; Peri et al., 2009). This message echoes the RoI's No Secrets report (DH, 2009: 13) which stated that safeguarding requires empowerment and that empowerment is everybody's business and not just confined to the concerns of older people.

Reworking for global mindedness: This example highlights that protection is not only limited to risk assessment and rescue but is rather embedded in broader human rights concerns for older people. Furthermore, elder abuse is not an isolated issue but has to be considered in the social context of older people's lives in society.

The needs of older persons go beyond simply 'protection' needs. Working with older persons requires an understanding of the social context of their lives and their agency. Furthermore, it is the stigmatised status of being old, vulnerable and incapable that needs to be addressed. It is also important to apply interventions based on an understanding of needs and wants that are situated in the living realities of 'vulnerable persons'. Understanding older peoples' ways of knowing and doing is therefore a priority to inform international, national and local policy (Dominelli, 2010). This example highlights how the whole range of human rights issues are interconnected and need to be realised in an integrative manner, rather than focussing only on individual needs rather than societal and community relations.

Ageism is a global issue that finds particular expression in local contexts. While social workers need to operate within the local context, it is important to contextualise the local experiences of ageism within the broader socio-economic political structures in which ageism is reproduced. The care of older people in traditional societies relied on families in communities. With increasing globalisation, and mobility induced by globalisation, economic forces have fractured traditional systems of care leading to isolation of older people and exposing them to risk of abuse. Globalisation, on the other hand, has also facilitated research resulting in international definition and indicators of abuse. The agency of older persons, however, should not be overlooked. Technology can provide creative ways to enable older persons to practice their agency and is increasingly used to provide alternative systems of support and to facilitate familial contact. Furthermore, paid care of older people is often provided by migrants, whose ideas and attitudes to older people may be different from those of local people. Furthermore, this care provision can also interplay with the politics of identity and race in local contexts. Thus, global and international ideas begin to shape local experiences and local provision of services. These ideas need to be carefully considered and analysed in terms of designing services and enabling users and service providers to understand needs and to work together.

Questions:

- Consider the local attitudes, and the global attitudes, toward ageism. For example, at what age do you think people should retire, if at all? What would the consequences of your suggested retirement age be for your society?
- How has internal and international migration and a globalised labour force impacted the lives of older people in your community?
- Are there mechanisms to ensure that the voices of older persons and their carers (including paid carers) are heard? What are the mechanisms or strategies used to promote individual agency?

Approaches to Protection

Approaches to protection work have very much been influenced by the theories and issues prevalent in western contexts, in particular notions of childhood and parenting. For example, attachment theory has been criticised for disregarding local contexts and historical socio-economic realities. International organisations such as the UN and UNICEF often endorse western ideas and promote their application in non-western countries (Abebe and Bessell, 2011; Laird, 2012). Notions of childhood and parenting are neither universal nor fixed. Abebe and Bessel (2011) offer a strong critique of the current understandings of childhood as being Eurocentric, and not taking into account the experiences other parts of the world. The western notion of childhood is conceptualised as an 'age of play and education' rather than 'work', which is contrary to many cultures where children work and where children's work is inter-woven into the fabric of family life, culture and society. Tower's (1996) research shows how African–American families expect all members of the family to work, and contribute in some way to the family's resources, which should not be construed as neglect or child labour. Clearly, ideas about childhood, the roles of family members and parenting practices also differ around the world (Rose and Meezan, 1996; Morelli et al., 1992). For example, in many developed countries, emphasis is placed on privacy, independence and self-reliance. In western countries, many families expect infants to learn to sleep on their own. In other cultures, this is something that would be considered neglectful (Morelli et al., 1992). The understanding of who *should* and who *can* protect vulnerable children also differs. In most cultures, it is generally the family and related extended family members who are responsible for 'protecting' children. Most cultures have informal networks, arrangements and strat-egies to enable this. The Maori welfare system use the Family Group Conference (FGC) as a strategy to resolve issues arising in families. The FGC is a unique strategy in that it recognises that the family needs support but also upholds the right of families and friends to address arising issues. A FGC is a conference that is held within the family to which extended family relatives, close friends and well-wishers can also be invited. At the FGC, the problem that the family is facing, as well as ideas and resources to address the problem, are discussed. The family is thus able to activate their own resources and deal with the problem within their larger family and community context. FGCs also enable provision of care and resources for children within their own cultural contexts that is familiar to the children. FGC is based on the assumption that families know best and have the best interests of their own children at heart. Research also shows that children growing up in families that they are related or close to, or in stable long-term placements, fare better in education, employment, and health outcomes than children in institutions or foster care (ElHage, 2016). The Care Crisis Review report also recognised the need to support families rather than taking children into care (ADCS, 2018). However, from a global mindedness approach, one should always be mindful that no single strategy can provide a universal solution and what works in one context may not work in another. Furthermore, it remains important to give space to communities and families to express their ways of dealing with problems rather than imposing methods and interventions that may not be relevant or culturally appropriate.

Example 3.2

Protection Work and Indigenous Practices (New Zealand)

Identifying the issues: It is widely acknowledged that families are the best places for the care of children. Efforts are made in most developed countries to support families to care for their children and even in cases where children have to be removed from their families, foster families or kinship placements are sought. In countries such as New Zealand, the traditional Maori model of resolving problems within families through family group conferencing is legally mandated before care proceedings are initiated. FGCs have also become popular in other countries such as the UK, USA and Australia as a way of working with families and helping them to resolve problems and issues concerning children (Barn and Das, 2015).

In other countries, such as Ghana and India, residential care systems are still in place. Most social workers and organisations in these countries are working toward developing policies and systems of care for children in families and dismantling residential care systems.

Critical analysis: When residential systems were introduced in the 19th century, they were believed to provide improved care for children in troubled families. Child welfare history in New Zealand, Australia, Canada and the USA shows how indigenous families were regarded as inferior and children were forcibly removed from these families to be raised in orphanages and residential care. Other families from minority groups have also often been treated in a similar manner. In previously colonised countries, such as Ghana, residential care was introduced to accommodate neglected, abused and vulnerable children. The socio-economic realities of previously colonial countries, meant that traditional family systems were destroyed. Furthermore, poverty has resulted in contemporary rural–urban migration, and the subsequent demise of the extended family has led to a dearth of resources and infrastructure for child care. Furthermore, pandemics, famines and diseases such as HIV/AIDS in many countries have resulted in many children becoming orphans. In many such cases, residential care introduced during colonial times continues to be offered as the primary alternative to care by one's own genetic family.

However, strategies such as FGCs, aimed at enabling families to collectively resolve their own problems, may not be applicable elsewhere. An exploration of FGCs among Bangladeshi minority groups in London indicated that migrant families lacked the extended family support required for group counselling to be effective (Barn and Das, 2015). In addition, families were also concerned about their private matters being exposed to their relatives and friends which they experienced as stigmatising.

Reworking for global mindedness: From a global mindedness approach, it is important to understand service provision systems from historical and cultural perspectives. In the case of FGCs, while they offer a good model of practice, they can often become difficult to implement for migrant families who are geographically scattered and may not have the local familial networks and traditional support systems. Similarly, it may be more important to ensure good residential care for children with appropriate staff and infrastructures to support families before advocating a complete break from residential care. In many contexts, residential care with regular contact with families can be a viable alternative. Different variations of resolving issues within families and communities also exist in other communities and this local knowledge and experience should not be disregarded.

The consideration of local social work interventions in a global context may offer opportunities for innovation and practice development. However, the cultural or political currency of translating new ideas into different cultural and social contexts should be approached with cultural sensitivity. While FGC, as outlined in this case study, is increasingly acknowledged as an international method of social work intervention (Barn and Das, 2015), its application may have to be adapted to different contexts by considering the unique needs of clients in their communities, cultural practices and the availability of the appropriate infrastructure. FGCs developed from a practice within Maori communities by seeking to enable and empower families. FGCs for migrant groups with few social networks, may be challenging to implement and might require extensive adaptations and different resources and skills. Global mindedness in practice offers a critical perspective for understanding the complexity issues relating to cultural universalism and relativism in social work practice.

Questions:

- How would you negotiate human rights at the level of the individual, at the level of the family, at the level of the community in protection work?
- How have theories and practices of child welfare and protection changed over the last 50 years?
- How would you include differences in cultural practices and expectations with regards to child care in the context of protection?

Navigating Protection Work Across Global and Local Contexts

The Human Rights Convention (HRC) as well as associated conventions reflects the broadest and most widely accepted mandate in terms of rights of adults and children. These provide guidelines and ideas as to what must be protected. The UN monitors progress made with regards to protecting human rights in most countries and identifies priority areas for further work. Most signatory countries are required to frame their laws in ways which are consistent with the HRC and other conventions to which countries have signed up to. However, not all western countries have signed up to the major conventions; for example, the USA is not a party to the United Nations Convention on the Rights of the Child (UNCRC). This has implications in terms of how an issue is addressed in national or global terms. It also affects joint working and the foundation on which cooperations and interventions can take place. Furthermore, countries have different national laws and systems in place that ultimately determine the individual country's interpretation and level of commitment to these conventions. For example, UNCRC defines a child as a person below the age of 18. However, many countries have different permissible age limits in terms of when children can be employed, may be married, may consent to sex, and be held responsible for criminal activities, ranging from 7 years to 18 years of age.

Even though it may be clear who needs to be protected and how they should be protected, protection work in practice is more complex and depends on the weighing of risks and available alternatives. The social, historical, economic and political context shapes the nature of risks involved, the availability of alternatives and options, and ultimately the role and responsibilities of the protection workers involved. In the case study, below, we highlight the issue of rescuing child sex workers in the UK and India. Different contextual realities that shape the alternatives and risks, determining the roles of social workers in such rescue work are discussed.

> **Example 3.3**
>
> ## Differing Roles of Social Workers (India, UK)
>
> *Identifying the issues*: Both India and the UK, are signatories to the UNCRC and have legislation to protect children from harm. Social work in the UK is legislated and social work involvement in child protection issues is clearly defined. In fact, the emphasis on the paramountcy of the wellbeing of the child in the UK mandates that social workers intervene within families, sometimes with the help of other formal agencies (such as police), which may result in the removal of children from families if they are deemed as living in harmful and exploitative conditions. Indian legislation also aims to protect children from abuse, neglect and rejection. However, Indian social workers do not have the legal powers to rescue children they may believe to be at risk and have limited resources and legal mandate to investigate such cases. Investigations when abuse is suspected are mostly a matter for police and probation officers (who may not be social workers). The systems, in terms of how police and social workers cooperate and who has the responsibility and power to act, are thus different in the UK and in India. The living conditions in both countries are also vastly different, which in turn shapes the cultural approaches, resources and prioritisation of different rights. Despite the different roles, both social workers in the UK and in India aim to achieve best outcomes for children by uniting them with their families and supporting families to care for children. Furthermore, social workers in both contexts advocate for children's rights and aim to provide opportunities for children to express their views.
>
> Social workers in the UK aim to ensure the overall wellbeing of children and may remove children from their homes

and place them into care if they are considered to be at risk. However, Indian social workers facing similar situations may place greater emphasis on improving the overall conditions of children within their current context rather than placing them in care or suggesting further investigations, unless there is strong evidence of abuse.

The difference in these two approaches is a reflection of the context and legislation orientation to vulnerability and care. The UK context clearly aims to protect children and prioritises their protection above all else. In this sense the system is individualistic and focusses on the child in need. In India, on the other hand, the system is not top down and aims to protect children within their environments and emphasises their relationships in families and to their carers. This is not to suggest that social workers in the UK would not try to support better integration of the child into the family. For example, social workers working with sex workers in red light areas in India often come across children living in spaces used by their mothers for sex work. In the UK, this could present enough risk to initiate an investigation about the child's welfare. However in India, social workers act to provide alternative spaces for socialisation for children (when their mothers work) and aim to educate mothers to help them better protect their children. In many non-governmental organisations (NGOs), social workers have also identified children employed in the sex trade and rather than initiate a rescue attempt, social workers have worked with the children to first prepare them for rescue and then liaise with the police to carry out rescue operations. In this way, social workers have sought the participation of the children, and their right to a family, as fundamental to their practice. In operations to rescue minor sex workers, consideration is given to alternatives for the child after rescue. As sex work is highly stigmatised, there is often little acceptance of children who were once involved in sex work back into their communities. Furthermore, there are often limited opportunities and alternatives for rescued children in the community and they are often lured back to return to sex work.

On the other hand, rescuing children in sex work can be considered rather straightforward in the UK, irrespective if the child wants to be rescued or not. The socio-economic contexts in the UK as well as attitudes toward childhood and sex differ, making rescue and rehabilitation quite different in comparison to India.

Critical analysis: From a global mindedness approach, the roles and responsibilities of social workers in India and the UK can only be understood when one understands the local realities of practice. India is an emerging civic, democratic society and social workers see their roles as agents of change within this context. They are orientated toward promoting social and economic changes so that issues of poverty and exploitation can be addressed. These are considered as key causes that render children vulnerable. Social workers in India thus share a positive image and are often seen as supporting families and children. In the UK, on the other hand, due to an extensive welfare system, concerns related to children are not located within larger societal issues but within individual contexts. Social workers see their role as supporting individual families and children. Due to their statutory powers and employment by the State, social workers are often seen as agents of the State. The focus on the paramountcy of the children's needs emphasises the involvement of social worker on behalf of the child rather than for the family. Children's rights are often prioritised over parental rights. Social work interventions are thus often less welcomed by families, particularly in relation to interventions in child protection.

Furthermore, in the UK, attitudes toward sex, opportunities for women as well as notions of childhood are different as compared to India. It can be argued that the implications of the stigma of sex work is less in the UK than in India. In addition, there is an inherent assumption in the UK that the society will and can support children. However, notions of childhood are different in the Indian context. Concerns about protecting children of sex workers as well as the children rescued from sex work are present in both contexts but dealing with the risks present for these two groups is handled differently in the UK and in India. This is reflected in the particular ways in which social workers respond to child protection cases and the strategies they employ to protect children.

Reworking for global mindedness: From a global mindedness approach it is important to understand the different country and culture specific contexts. It is also vital to acknowledge that there is constant exchange and adaptability of ideas across contexts. In the UK, there seems to be an increasing focus on communities, such as service provision in communities and by community members and organisations (see ACDS, 2018). Similarly, social workers in India are also working toward a work environment with clearer defined roles for social work and increased status and legislative power. While people involved in social work practice in India and the UK can learn from each other, the simple transfer of ideas from one context to another should be resisted, as it can be damaging to local communities and local ways of doing things.

Questions:

- What do you think are common principles in protecting children? What are the differences across cultures?
- What do you think are the structural factors which shape the role and function of social work practice in your country?
- Identify any particular social work approach or a case in protection work. What knowledge and skills would be necessary for you to apply this approach to similar cases in another country?

Protection Work and Competing Rights

Protection work involves both supportive and coercive interventions. Social workers find themselves negotiating the rights of adults, individuals and communities which are not always congruent with the rights of children. The main sources of tension are the rights and wishes of the family and those of the child. From a broader social or cultural perspective, some societies promote the rights and sanctity of the family through legislation, while other countries consider the rights of the child as paramount. The prioritising of rights is critically important in determining the focus of the child welfare system, the preferred methods of intervention and the allocation of resources.

In countries such as the UK and Australia, child protection workers have been openly criticised by the media and general public for failing to adequately protect children in ways that have led to the abuse of, and in some cases the death of, the child. You may be aware of such cases of child or elder abuse in your own country that have attracted media attention and public debate. There is no clear consensus as to which rights should be upheld and which rights compromised when faced with issues where the rights of the different actors involved seemingly compete with each other. Cultural ideas as well as historical issues play a very significant role in which rights are to be considered most primary. We consider the following case study of adoption as a method of seeking 'permanence' (permanent placement for children in care) to further explore these differences.

Example 3.4

Adoption as a Method for Seeking Permanency for Children in Need (Global)

Identifying the issues: Protecting vulnerable children is central to protection work internationally. Children may become wards of the State when their biological families are unable to provide appropriate care. Care and parenting of children is then temporarily taken over by the State. These children are 'looked after' children. In extreme cases, when all possibilities to address the risk within the family at that point in time have been exhausted, child care is totally taken over by the State. This is generally a last resort intervention that is only used in extreme cases (Kelly and Das, 2012). Almost all countries have mechanisms to identify children at risk and ways to intervene on behalf of children. We consider the pathways to permanence of 'looked after' children in different countries to highlight the similarities and differences in practice, and the underlying assumptions of practice.

Vulnerable, neglected or orphaned children are sometimes adopted with a view to offering them better lives than local care homes or foster care can offer. Generally, adoption within their own country is preferred but children have been placed for international adoption when this has not been possible. This has invited much criticism, and sometimes leads to the sale of babies across borders and the development of adoption of children as a business. In addition, adoption of children across countries also presents issues of identity and belonging for adopted children, particularly when they become older (Mapp et al., 2008). However, within-country adoption of 'looked after' children also presents issues that require consideration that we outline below.

In spite of the evidence that adoption is a positive intervention for children, adoption as a pathway to permanence for 'looked after' children is used differently across countries. In the UK, USA and Israel, adoption, even without parental consent, is possible. However, in other countries such as Spain, adoption of 'looked after' children without parental consent is not legally permissible. Similarly, adoptions of Aboriginal children in Australia and the USA are governed by particular legal caveats. Adoption of Aboriginal children without consent or to non-aboriginal families in these countries often requires special consideration. In Romania, due to large number of children in orphanages, international adoption was popular but was banned in the 1990s to stop the misuse and sale of children.

Critical analysis: Our analysis in this section considers the reasons for the differential use of adoption across countries to better understand these differences rather than merely comparing the availability or non-availability of adoption as a pathway to permanence. Practices in the adoption of children are guided by assumptions about the care of children, the rights of the family, historical contexts and socio-economic realities. In countries where adoption, even without parental consent is possible, emphasis is placed on the welfare of children and their need for a stable and permanent family. In Spain, the high emphasis on parental rights provides the bedrock for Spanish legal structures, making adoption without parental consent not possible but instead encouraging long-term foster care. In the USA and Australia, the historical injustices of the welfare system against aboriginal families have resulted in stricter controls to ensure that Aboriginal families and cultures do not face further discrimination, through laws that are specially applied to these communities. Furthermore, adoption in Aboriginal communities is a very foreign and culturally alien idea (Stonehouse, 1992; Legal Services Commission of South Australia, 2018). Finally, the misuse of the adoption system in Romania that forced many children with families into orphanages and wrongful international adoptions had resulted in a ban to stop the sale of babies.

Reworking for global mindedness: While there is no one correct way of practice, it is nevertheless interesting to note how countries acknowledge the importance of families as the best care system for children and strive to achieve this for 'looked after' children.

It is important that social workers need to consider the core principles of human rights, and implement practices and strategies that reflect these consideration of rights. Human rights can only be truly realised in the particular cultural and social context of people's lives. From a global minded perspective, any adaptation of global standards should first consider the local positions and contexts rather than imposing them. This means adapting global standards and procedures to local ways of perceiving and doing things. There are various contrasting approaches to address issues. The unequal power of globalisation often pushes for global ideas to be adopted in local contexts. It remains important to ensure that global exchange and comparison does not lead to loss of diversity and homogenisation. Global mindedness requires the consideration of various approaches and the engagement in a process of dialogue, adaptability and change between the local and the global to ensure that the local and the global can dynamically co-exist.

Questions:

- How do the rights of asylum-seeking children and their families compare to that of children of citizens in your country?
- How would you ensure an informed consideration of the various human rights guarantees, with respect to children and their families from minority cultures (given that their social, cultural and economic context may differ from the majority culture)?
- what are your views on promoting fostering or adoption of children by families who share kinship ties with the child or have similar cultural or ethnic background as the child in question?

Summary

In this chapter, we have identified a number of approaches to protection work in different contexts. For example, definitions of child and elder abuse differ across different legal and cultural jurisdictions, despite the existence of international conventions and definitions. Thresholds of tolerance and State intervention also differ considerably from one country to another. The case studies analysed highlight that the universal conventions and human rights must to be considered and can be applied in relation to cultural and historical contexts.

We have also discussed social workers' capacities and functions in protection work. Protection work is inherently controversial and raises questions on the definition of vulnerability. What factors determine the need for support and protection? What actions are possible and desired for protection are, of course, dependent on the cultural orientations of people and the historical, social and economic realities of a community. Furthermore, social workers' roles are also defined by the organisational, social cultures, histories and economic contexts within which they operate. From a global minded perspective, we have tried to highlight the need to understand these approaches in context. Global minded social workers are reminded to avoid making simple comparisons across practice contexts but analyse and critically ask how these contexts shape practice (how are practices different and why are they different?). Analysing these questions in contrast to one's own practice can also be very useful to highlight our own hidden assumptions and to regard regular practice issues critically.

Global mindedness in protection work therefore requires knowledge of both international and national legal frameworks, human rights and the capacity to critically self-reflect upon one's own assumptions together, and the implications (reflexivity) in praxis. Protection work is linked to diversity, structural and sustainability work. Global mindedness in such work requires an open mind to be able to consider different possibilities, to allow room and consideration of the various roles that history, culture and contemporary realities play in shaping particular arguments and ways of thinking and doing. However, the challenge of global mindedness is to be able to learn from each other and to engage in exchange in a critical manner so that the global and the local critically and productively engage with one another.

It is perhaps within the context of protection work that it becomes clear that social work is informed by the humanities and social sciences. While, on the one hand, social workers aim for evidence-informed or evidence-based practice, decisions are not only based on rational thought processes but also are shaped by humanitarian values, ideas of justice and perceptions of history. Decision making in practice goes beyond reliance on rational and scientific paradigms. Our humanity, ideas of social justice, historical cultural influences and historical events play a significant role in shaping what we consider good or ideal. Global mindedness enables a better recognition of diversity, different realities, as well as possibilities for action, while at the same time, highlighting human rights as a source of guidance in practice.

4 Global Mindedness and Diversity Work

Introduction

In all countries, social workers work with the marginalised, the ignored, the stigmatised, the oppressed or the discriminated people in society (Gaine, 2010). Social work is essentially about challenging inequality and oppression by advocating for equality, promoting diversity, social integration and positive social change. Therefore social work has always been concerned with diversity work. Early examples of diversity work included the settlement movements in the USA and parts of Europe developed by pioneering social workers in the early 20th Century to address the poverty and inequality resulting from rapid industrialisation and the international and internal migration of people. Social workers used the issues of child and family poverty to educate society and governments on the need for major structural and welfare reform to achieve equality within society. They skillfully combined diversity, protection and structural work. More recently the increase in forced migration across international borders, i.e. refugees, asylum seekers and political and economic immigrants, has yet again highlighted the importance of diversity work. The international definition of social work explicitly refers to concepts such as empowerment, liberation, social justice, human rights and diversity. Global mindedness involves an acknowledgement of difference and a commitment to work with diversity for social justice through creative and transformative social change.

What Is Diversity Work?

Diversity work refers to social work intervention with individuals or groups of people who, because of their gender, sexuality, class, ethnicity, physical or intellectual abilities, culture, or religion, are often discriminated against and excluded by society. Difference is often used as a justification for the inequitable treatment of people and the denial of their basic human rights. A central concept in diversity work is addressing *othering*.

Othering is the process of differentiating those that are thought to be different from oneself or the mainstream. While this is a very common social phenomenon, it tends to reinforce and reproduce positions of domination and subordination in society (Thompson, 2016). Dominance often leads to oppression, where select groups are systematically discriminated against based on their difference.

Ideas of dominance and 'otherness' are often nurtured by stereotypes, discrimination, racial biases and prejudices. Within every society, social interactions and relations divide people into dominant/superior and subordinate/inferior categories. Two of the most notorious examples of othering leading to political domination are the apartheid system in South Africa, where access to political power and resources was based on racial divisions, i.e. being black, coloured or white, and racial segregation of people in South Africa, as well as the racial segregation of African–Americans in the USA. These relations of domination consist of the systematic devaluing of the attributes and contributions of those deemed inferior and their exclusion from the social resources available to those in the dominant group. While this interaction can be a source of inspiration and exchange, it can also be a source of conflict and precipitate violence. Attacks on persons of different religion, gender, different sexuality and race, as well as violent resistances by discriminated groups are examples of such violence. Discrimination occurs at different levels, i.e. personal (othering, victim blaming, prejudice, stereotypes), cultural (markers of inclusion, exclusion, beliefs in superiority of one culture over another, discrimination) and structural (social division, inequitable disruption of and access to power, wealth and material resources). The goal of diversity work is to address not only discriminatory practices but also the conditions that reproduce discrimination. The transformation of diversity and difference into a positive asset to be valued is a positive expression of diversity work. Social diversity moves beyond merely tolerating difference, to respecting, appreciating, understanding, engaging and promoting difference. In order to address discrimination and oppression, social workers are required to work across the three levels of the personal, cultural and the structural levels of society. Working with refugees, unemployed people, older people, people with a mental illness, or LGBT (Lesbian Gay Bisexual Transgender) communities, involves engaging in some form of diversity work addressing discrimination or even oppression. Diversity work is built on the belief that people feel most included in society when they feel most valued and that their individual or group differences are accepted (Walker, 1994: 212) and represents a basic principle of global mindedness.

Equality is both a value and an outcome of diversity work. Equality is primarily about fairness and is linked closely to concepts such as citizenship (Turner, 1986), social justice and human rights. An important point to remember is that equality is not just about treating people the same. It must be recognised that not all people start with the same opportunities at birth. Some have more power, status and privilege than others depending on gender, class, physical and mental ability, ethnicity and so on. The Marmott Review (2010) into health inequalities in England provided startling evidence demonstrating how social determinants of health, such as where one is born, grows up, lives, or works, determines health and wellbeing and results in health and social inequalities.

Basic categories of equality include political equality (civic equality, equality before the law), equality of outcome or result (income and wealth), equality of opportunity (access to resources, schools, political platforms), equality of treatment (agency and responsibility) and equality of membership in society (citizenship). Social work aims to promote a just society by challenging injustice and valuing diversity. A just society exists when all people share a common humanity and therefore have a right to equitable treatment, support for their human rights and a fair allocation of community resources. The aims of diversity, protection and structural work therefore intersect.

Diversity work is wide-ranging and sometimes controversial or confronting. It encourages the maximisation of everyone's potential and allows for intervention at the personal, organisational and structural level. Acceptance of diversity may be challenging as it requires individuals to acknowledge and negotiate differences in order to establish commonalities. This process lies at the very core of global minded practice. Negotiating difference constructively requires engaging with and dealing with inequality and conflict positively.

A word of warning, there is a tendency in diversity work to over-simplify working with difference, by either making it exotic or underestimating its impact. This then leads to problematic ways of acknowledging or dealing with difference that are superficial, tokenistic and do not address core issues. For example, Aboriginal art has become highly commercial as white Australians and Europeans have come to appreciate the originality of indigenous arts. As a consequence of the commercialisation of Aboriginal art, some individual Aboriginal artists have been subject to exploitation. Historically, most of the profits from the sales of expensive Aboriginal artwork have gone to white Australians. The artwork has been exoticised and its original significance to aboriginal cultural and spiritual meaning is lost.

Sometimes extreme forms of political correctness can result in the further and sometimes complete denial of difference. For example, the Troubles[1] in Northern Ireland often led to a situation of heightened

---

[1] A period of 30 years of protracted conflict between Protestants and Catholics in Northern Ireland, ending with the signing of the Good Friday Agreement in 1998.

sensitivity to identity where asking about a person's ethnic, cultural or religious background in Northern Ireland was highly charged. This often led to an avoidance of dealing with issues of sectarianism and attempting a seemingly neutral approach to provision of services. Only recently has the past experiences of sectarianism been openly explored with both Catholic and Protestant social work students in the university classroom (Campbell et al. 2013). Providing students with formal spaces and opportunities to discuss their political, religious and social differences helps to facilitate open dialogue and promote global mindedness in future social workers.

The following diagram highlights the various aspects of diversity work. The concepts of equality, power, justice, culture, inclusiveness and difference are linked and central in diversity work and global mindedness in practice (Figure 4.1).

Diversity work involves addressing issues of inclusion through positively promoting and valuing difference. This requires engagement with minority communities as well as dominant power groups for a better understanding and negotiation of power so as to address privilege and disadvantage. Again, this informs our understanding as to the aims of global mindedness.

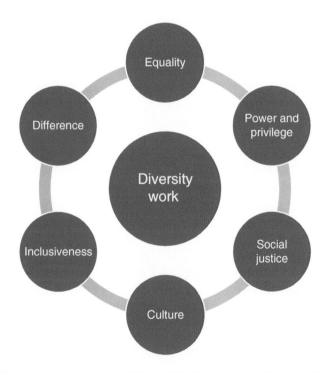

Figure 4.1 A Summary of Global Mindedness and Diversity Work

Cultural and Religious Diversity

Recognition of difference and how to work with culture in the context of day-to-day practice is fundamental to diversity work. Hall (1959) defines culture as the way of life of a people: the sum of their learned behaviour patterns, attitudes and material things. Most cultural aspects or nuances are primarily subconscious and represent an invisible control mechanism operating our thoughts and actions. A useful analogy is that of culture as a computer program that guides the actions, communication and responses of people in their everyday lives. Ironically, we often only become aware of culture when we are exposed to a different culture. Culture in itself is not a fixed entity but is constantly developing over time. Whether a particular object, idea, thought or point of view belongs to one culture is not a question of culture but rather to which historical point one is referring too; for example, the question as to whether 'Chicken Tikka Masala' is part of British culture (Cook, 2001). Chicken Tikka masala is a british take of a recipe influenced by Indian cuuisine. A more appropriate question may be to ask at what point, and how, 'Chicken Tikka curry' became part of British culture. One could then argue that Chicken Tikka curry was not part of British culture in the 1900s but is indeed part of its culture today. This kind of reframing demonstrates the fluidity of culture as well the importance of fringe cultures on the broader cultural repertoire. It enables one to regard culture as fluid rather than fixed, and to recognise the various fringe elements that represent the multiplicity and diversity within every culture. Societal changes such as famines, migrations, and conquests have played a significant role in what we consider to be our culture today and that this has always been changing. In this sense, we are both products of culture but also creators of culture and our responses and reactions to historical developments shape our cultures.

It is impossible to talk about culture and not include religion. Religion has shaped culture, everyday practices and has played an instrumental role in determining social and political power. For example, the Bible in part documents the tensions between Judaism and Christianity the religious crusades are testament to the extent to which religion was used as a marker of difference, competition and animosity. As previously mentioned, religion was one of the factors contributing to conflict and division in Northern Ireland between Protestants and Catholics. It is clear that in Northern Ireland, the religious aspect is inextricably linked to historical politics and social inequality.

Religion plays a significant role in defining culture but this role is often exaggerated and similarities and differences between cultures (independent of religion) are often ignored or minimised. Through social, political and cultural mechanisms, religion is used as a basis for seemingly non-negotiable differences. In contemporary times, religion is increasingly used to emphasise identity, belongingness and community. More recently, the arrival of significant numbers of refugees of Muslim faith to extensively Christian European countries has become a source of tension within countries such as Finland, Germany, Hungary and France. Fear of difference, sometimes talked about under the pretext of religious extremism and radicalisation as a threat to national security, have contributed to public sentiments of social exclusion, and racism. We explore this in the following case study.

Example 4.1

Working for Religious Diversity (Europe)

Identifying the issues: Global mindedness involves new ways of working with religious diversity. The Human Rights Convention (HRC) clearly outlines that every individual has the freedom of conscience and religion. However, enabling this freedom and associated practices has often led to tensions. Most countries have particular norms based on the religion of the majority population that often lead to unequal treatment of people who practice other religions. These norms can be observed in everyday situations. If we consider Europe, where the Christian tradition is dominant and played a significant role in the development of Europe, religious aspects are visible in everyday contexts such as Sunday as the day of rest or weekly holiday, Christmas celebrations and national holidays. People of other faiths, however, are not offered similar treatment in terms of being able to take days off from work for religious observances.

The wearing of the headscarf and the practice of dressing modestly for Muslim women has generated much controversy in recent times. Many European countries have introduced petitions, laws and legislative restraints against headscarves and the 'Burkha' that fully covers Muslim women's faces and bodies. The main argument against these practices is the concern over the 'oppression of women'. This issue is particularly controversial in France, where some women have been fined for wearing the Burkini (a swimsuit that covers the whole body) on the beach. On the other hand, some French schools have supplied Muslim girls with Burkinis to enable their participation in swimming classes.

The gender segregation of Muslim men and women in mosques and separate codes of behaviour have further fuelled the gender debate leading to arguments that claim that Muslim women are suppressed or that, within Muslim communities, women do not have the same rights as men.

Critical analysis: It is clear that as social workers, we strive for gender equality. However, there is no basis for claiming that a woman in a bikini is more equal than a woman in a Burkini. Women face discrimination in various aspects of their lives and it is more likely that Christian and Muslim women share more similarities than differences in terms of the discrimination they face. Furthermore, other factors such as migration history, poverty and access to education tend to combine to increase the oppression for women, and religion is rarely the sole reason. At a group or community level, the political nuances of identifying as Muslim influences how and why women choose to cover their head or wear the Burkha. For many women, wearing the Burkha can be more a conscious act of resistance or solidarity with the group they identify with rather than a passive acceptance of oppression. Bilge (2010) has discussed this in his paper, arguing that many Muslim community members may understand these practices in terms of resisting imperialist oppression, or the capitalistic/gender exploitation of women. Yegenoglu (1998) and El Guindi (1999) have often discussed the use of the veil as women's resistance against Islamophobia. Muslim women may be strategically more interested in prioritising their identity struggles as Muslims and part of the minorities in the broader community rather than familial or patriarchal oppression. The recognition of the agency of women is extremely important, particularly in discourses on women's oppression.

Reworking for global mindedness: From a global minded approach, the wearing of the Burkha or head scarf has implications at the level of the personal and group. At one level the Burkha could be a symbol of resistance in response to perceived oppression, a matter of personal choice or a religious practice for Muslim women. In the local context head scarves may simply be the cultural norm. Differences in understanding of 'what the norm is' and 'what the accepted norm should be', has led to heated debates. However, there is clearly a need to engage with the dialogue based on rational arguments, consideration of different positionalities and a willingness to explore creative ways of addressing core issues such as women's rights and empowerment. The issue of women's oppression is a global issue and not one particular to Muslims. Women in western Christian societies and eastern Muslim societies experience both abuse and freedom. Global mindedness requires social workers to acknowledge the multiple positionalities that women occupy and give women the freedom to express themselves within their cultural frameworks. It would indeed be sad and unethical if the only feminist arguments were that of western women. Women in other countries also have feminist ideas but may choose to express them differently or choose a different path to emancipation. Women's empowerment is a universal goal but how it looks in specific contexts and cultures is culturally relevant. Without relevance in local contexts, the terms of rights and empowerment have little value or meaning.

Furthermore, for a global mindedness approach, it is essential that social workers also foster dialogue rather than simply take a side or promote binary arguments. Difference can only be accepted and celebrated when there are opportunities to challenge and to be challenged. Public spaces for critical discourse are often missing, resulting in dialogue that is one sided and categorical, and does not reflect the reality of people's lives.

Questions

- Can religion play a positive role in enabling human rights?
- How does your religion contribute to the oppression of women? What are the similarities and differences between the contexts and conditions with women from other religions?
- How can concerns about religious radicalisation and perceived threats to society be addressed?

Gender and Diversity

Feminism in the late 1960s played a significant role in the professions engagement with sexism, patriarchy and in understanding gendered dimensions of social work practice (Orme, 2002). Patriarchy refers to a system of social, political and economic arrangements which gives privilege and power to men over women. A diversity approach in social work practice aims to recognise how gender affects material resources, life changes and experiences for both men and women. The social work profession, in spite of its commitment to diversity and gender equality, experiences the reproduction of gender inequality within its own ranks. Thus, in most social work organisations gender inequality continues to be widespread. While the majority of social workers are women, men disproportionately occupy more management positions (Dahlkild-Öhman and Eriksson, 2013; Harlow, 2004). Significant pay differences within social work, with men earning more than women (Anastas, 2007), remains an economic reality even in post-industrialised countries such as the UK, Australia and Japan. These gendered positions in society thus very much shape organisational systems and services in social work, and limit the possibilities for transformative practice.

Disregarding gender inequality in the social care workforce leads to further inequalities such as the disregarding of service users' needs or gender blindness. Christie (2006) describes organisation constellations where social work services are mostly provided by women, which can lead to the feminisation of social services. Ignoring gender issues can lead to the planning and delivery of services that do not appropriately consider risks and which can lead to further marginalisation and sexism. We present a case study that highlights the particular vulnerability of women and children in war, refugee crises and disasters as this is often overlooked. The example outlines how being blind to the implications of differences compromises the impact of international protection or relief aid.

Example 4.2

Gender Blindness and Disaster Aid (Thailand, Indonesia, Sri Lanka)

Identifying the issues: Global mindedness involves paying attention to the impact of factors such as gender in the provision of services. On 26 December 2004, a tsunami struck eight countries in Asia and five in Africa. While the full number will never be known, tens of thousands of people were reported dead in Sri Lanka, Thailand, India and Indonesia (UNSETR, 2005a). Women and children were over-represented in the death toll (Rees et al., 2005). However, international aid in the post-disaster period exposed women to a second wave of horror that did not originate from the natural disaster. The incidences of rape, gang rape, molestation and physical abuse of women and girls in the course of unsupervised rescue operations and during their residence in temporary shelters have been extensively reported (APWLD, 2005a, 2005b; Fletcher et al., 2005; Rees et al., 2005).

Critical analysis: In the camps' environment, the lack of privacy caused by temporary and shanty accommodation left women and children more exposed (UNSETR, 2005b, 2005c). The lack of separate toilets for men and women, the absence of lights in the camp at night and public bathing facilities contributed to the risk and occurrence of rape. Across the countries affected by the tsunami, there were also reports of women and girls being forced to trade sex for food. Furthermore, there were concerns about trafficking activities becoming increasingly widespread (AIDMI, 2005; Burns, 2005). Despite the prevalence of sexual abuse, there were few sexual and reproductive health services available in the aftermath of the tsunami. In many cases, victims and survivors were without support or medical care for injury and disease associated with sexual and gender-based violence (Pittaway and Bartolomei, 2005). There was clearly a lack of appropriate identification of needs and ability to develop responses quickly. Crisis management strategies need to incorporate these aspects of difference in their planning – not to privilege women but to acknowledge their particular vulnerabilities in situations like this.

Reworking for global mindedness: When considering issues of diversity in this situation, it is clear that natural calamities render all groups vulnerable. However, equal treatment for all does not ensure equality. This example illustrates how different groups of people can be vulnerable in different ways. The multiple structural and cultural oppressions that women face in almost all societies can further exacerbate issues of access, safety and security, particularly in crisis situations. It becomes necessary to consider issues of difference to foster development and protection of vulnerable groups of people whose unique needs cannot be addressed by a 'one size fits all' policy. To correct structural inequalities, 'positive discrimination' policies are in place for marginalised groups. Examples of positive discrimination policies include those focussed on African–Americans in the USA, persons from lower castes/ scheduled castes in India, 'widening access' to overcome the class and race divide in the UK, and women's participation in management levels in Germany. However, these measures have to be considered in context and in view of the histories of a particular people and societies. It is essential to engage in dialogue with others to develop policies and processes that are inclusive and considers the wider society at large. A critical understanding of equal opportunities is essential and not only must the social worker consider issues of gender but also how gender superimposes and intersects with class, ethnic status, ability, sexuality and so on. The close examination of the nexus between the local and global becomes critical in such work particularly as global trends can highlight certain groups and ignore others, which may not reflect the realities of peoples' lives in domestic contexts. For some countries, issues of incorporating minority groups may be more urgent than women's issues. This is not to say that minority issues should be prioritised over women's issues or the other way around but rather to understand the situational context in which these concerns are located and how the concerns of different groups intersect.

Questions

- What would enable a society to become truly inclusive for women? What conditions are necessary for sustainable inclusion?
- How do you work with the concept of diversity in your practice? How have global trends contributed to the discussions of diversity among your clients? How have your practices adapted to these changes?
- What strategies can be employed to avoid the unintended consequences of not addressing diversity issues in the context of community work?

Abilities Diversity

In most western countries, difference has been conceptualised using disability, health conditions or behaviour that deviate from what is socially constructed or perceived as the normal (Williams, 2006). The medical model has historically resulted in a preoccupation with treating difference as an individual pathology. The need to identify, treat (intervene) and fix a person who is assessed and labeled as sick, ill or unhealthy has tended to become the dominant approach to intervention. For example, in the USA homosexuality was considered deviant and therefore defined as a mental illness as recently as the1960s. It was not until the late 1980s that the diagnosis of a *sexual orientated disturbance* was deleted from the Diagnostic and Statistical Manual of Mental Disorders (DSM). The labelling of homosexuality as a mental health disorder reflected the religious beliefs and practices of the time. While the contribution of medicine is vital in addressing health issues, and in the prevention of some forms of disability and illness, the application of the medical model can also contribute to stigmatisation, disempowerment and discrimination of groups of people. In addition, the focus on the medicalisation process places the power to diagnose and treat illness and deviant behaviour firmly in the control of professional experts, thereby disempowering the individual and their priories, rights and choices. This type of thinking has served to generate negative views of people who have disabilities or different abilities and their status in society.

An alternative to the medicalisation of difference is the social model, which rejects the notion that disability is a characteristic of the individual. A person may have an impairment of bodily or mental function, but that only becomes a disability to the extent that society is not structured to include people who are different (Williams, 2006: 14). The United Nations Convention of the Rights of Persons with Disabilities reflects this view. From a global mindedness approach the role of social work is to challenge structural barriers which serve to exclude people and to empower individuals to exercise their rights. Significant gains have been made in the of disability rights as a consequence. More recently, the influence of neoliberal economics has meant that many western governments have withdrawn from the practice of direct service provision, preferring instead to tender out disability services to charitable or commercial interests. Alongside this development, there has been an international push for greater personalisation of services, giving people with disabilities increased choice in, and responsibility over, services received. More flexible and individualised services promote empowerment; however, it may be argued that the economic models underlying such changes in service delivery may not be appropriate or equitable for all individuals or contexts as revealed in the next case study.

Example 4.3

Choice in Services for People with Disabilities (UK, Republic of Ireland, Australia)

Identifying the problem: The challenges as to how to give people with disabilities choices in terms of how they use government payments to purchase care services have generated considerable debate and discussion among people with disabilities, professionals, politicians, policy makers and academics (Scourfield, 2005). Internationally, there are a variety of funding models for the provision of personal budgets, such as 'direct payments' in the UK (Spandler and Vick, 2006), 'consumer directed care' or 'self-directed care' in states of Australia (Fisher et al., 2010), and 'cash and counselling schemes' in the USA (Dale and Brown, 2006). The different approaches are understood as a continuum involving the relative levels of control between professionals and service users. On this continuum, professionally monitored models of service delivery occupy one end of this spectrum and the service-user directed model at the other.

Critical analysis: Global mindedness involves the questioning of global trends and analysis of evidence to inform changes to services. Personal budgets have undoubted given people with disabilities more control and choice over their lives, and have contributed to a better quality of life with more flexibility and satisfaction and real empowerment. However, in a large survey of people using personal budgets in the UK, Hatton and Waters (2011) reported mixed responses about the processes involved. Personal budget schemes can reduce control and oversight for some service user groups (Ungerson, 2004). Service user groups have criticised UK government plans to introduce personal budgets into healthcare as being too restrictive and bureaucratic in administration. Galpin and Bates (2009) point out that there are 'winners and losers' in every model of social care provision. Thus, service users who lack the essential attributes and support to make rational and strategic choices are less able to benefit from personal budgets compared to other groups. Those without the ability or capacity to manage personal budgets tend to be excluded from access to this type of funding, unless support (such as advocacy, financial assistance and protective policy/legislation) is in place to facilitate their participation. Personal budgets provide opportunities to enable people with significant cognitive disabilities to exercise their preferences, but they may also present unique challenges for supporting and communicating decision making.

Existing service providers may find the introduction of new market models and the prospect of having to 'sell' their care services somewhat challenging. For example, service providers in Australia have criticised their government for wanting control of agencies, but distancing themselves from the risks and responsibilities of service provision (Aged and Community Services, 2008). Furthermore, the introduction of personal budgets is thought, by some, to have the potential to increase opportunities for the misuse of funding or budget allocation difficulties.

Reworking for global mindedness: New global care philosophies are influencial and the introduction of personal budgets is one such example, along with examples of new models that seek to combine health and social care services. Many recent approaches to health and welfare services claim to be the solution to many of the failings of the welfare system and State such as the lack of individualised care, spiralling economic costs and the use of ineffective care interventions (Anand et al., 2018). Careful consideration must be given to the implications of new care philosophies and systems for diverse groups of users.

(Reproduced with permission from the National Disability Authority, Northern Ireland. Full version available online.)

Questions

- What are some of the economic and structural changes taking place in the provision of health and welfare services in your country?
- What are the local and global conditions that drive or restrict people with disabilities to have more control over the services provided? What are some of the advantages and risks involved?
- Who are the winners and losers in the personalisation of social care services? Does the availability of choice in a neo-liberal market allow the realisation of human rights for all?

Human Rights and Diversity

A human rights-based approach is arguable the most relevant practice theory for informing global mindedness in practice. The United Nations Charters on Human Rights provides the legal and social mandate for social work practice across the global north and south. It may be claimed that human rights are universal but the exercising of one person's rights can result in another person's marginalisation. For example, the right to freedom of speech is universal but when it results in racism and oppression, can it still be considered a right? Another difficulty with the human rights approach is that it tends to privilege legal rights at the expense of social and economic rights, which are just as important in achieving social justice particularly for minority and excluded groups. Ife and Fiske (2006) argue that legal rights mainly concern individuals and as such are the focus of lawyers, while social and economic rights are the work of social workers to be achieved through collective action.

Global minded social workers should be encouraged to consider the contradictions between local practices/cultural beliefs and universal human rights. Cultural practices toward the treatment of women and children may contradict social work ethics and universal human rights making local–global tensions characteristic of day-to-day social work practice a frequent reality. Such cultural practices are no longer confined by national borders as peoples' lives have become increasingly transnational. For example, the continuation of the practice of female genital cutting is controversial but continues in many countries, despite efforts to make it illegal. The following case study provides an opportunity to see this paradox using a global minded approach.

Example 4.4

Human Rights and Cultural Practices (UK, Africa, South Asia)

Identifying the issues: Female circumcision or female genital cutting is carried out in many different religions and countries throughout the world. It is recognised internationally as a violation of the human rights of girls and women, reflecting a deep-rooted inequality between the sexes, and constituting an extreme form of discrimination against women. It is nearly always carried out on minors and is a violation of the rights of children. The practice also violates a person's rights to health, security and physical integrity, the right to be free from torture and cruel, inhuman or degrading treatment, and the right to life when the procedure results in death (WHO, 2014). Despite human rights legislation and campaigns in Africa, Middle East and Europe the practice has not be eliminated. In the UK, a special campaign has been adopted to identify young girls from specific ethnic backgrounds who are considered at risk of being taken out of the UK to Asian and African countries for the procedure to be performed according to traditional practice. Examples of medical practitioners in western countries performing female genital cutting have also been reported to authorities in the UK and Canada. Such practices must be condemned. However, more critical questions as to why families, who love and respect their daughters, subject them to this practice? Such parents are not ignorant or brainwashed but influenced by very powerful social and cultural factors, that influence their decisions as to what they believe is in the best interest of their daughters.

Critical analysis: Explanations as to the continued prevalence of female genital cutting are complex and require an understanding of the dynamics of culture, religion and history in contemporary times. The practice of female genital cutting is entrenched in local patriarchal practices, and linked with the role and status of women, including the older women who often preform these procedures. The patterns and causes of female genital cutting and other forms of gendered violence are explained as a network of social, economic and legal norms and structures that function to maintain the compliance of families and younger women, and the accumulation of social capital by older women. The control of women's bodies, the reproduction of power over their behaviour and the adoption of self-surveillance may also be understood from a feminist or post-modernist perspective. The potential for women to be both the oppressed and the oppressor is reflected in a critical analysis of power. Wells (2012), however, suggests that the introduction of human rights legislation in African countries has resulted in female genital cutting being perceived as a medical or rights issue separate from the cultural, religious and gender context. Therefore, it is common in many African countries for female genital cutting to become the symbol of resistance against western or colonial influences and as a result, some girls and women willingly support FGC.

Reworking for global mindedness in practice: The human right based approach is arguably the most relevant practice theory for informing social work in response to female genital cutting. However, a more comprehensive and critical reading of the human rights agenda is prudent in order to understand the tensions between cultural and human rights. In many non-western countries, the human rights agenda has been historically used as an argument to make demands on local people and communities to adapt to global norms and trends. A difficulty with the human rights approach is that it tends to privilege legal rights at the expense of social, cultural and economic rights, which are just as important in achieving social justice, particularly for minority and excluded groups. Ife and Fiske (2006) argue that legal rights mainly concern individuals and as such are the focus of lawyers, while social and economic rights are the work of social workers to be achieved through bottom up approaches to collective and community action. The historical implications of colonisation and the top down application of human rights provides a useful analysis as to how and why oppressive cultural practices persist, and new forms of dominance and oppression are created. It is important to understand that dominant culture is never static and is always open to new influences and new ways of reproducing or resisting oppression. Interventions that have been effective in changing cultural and religious practices tend to be both participatory and developmental in their approach.

Questions
- From a social work perspective, how would you approach the argument between cultural versus other human rights?
- How does your analysis of female genital cutting inform your understanding of similar forms of gendered violence in other cultural contexts, i.e. breast augmentation, male circumcision?
- How could you remain sensitive to dominant cultural practices and perhaps accommodate religious and cultural practices?

Summary

Global mindedness in response to social inequality arising from difference and diversity involves identifying and linking global and local influences and negotiating change. The case studies have highlighted how the markers of difference i.e. gender, culture, religion, class, sexual identity intersect with one another, making the understanding of inequality complex. The inter-relationship between diversity work and the need for protection and structure change has also been illuminated by the examples outlined. Values of humanism and knowledge of the interrelationship between the local and global, as well as skills that enable working with diverse people across different levels such as intercultural competency, are necessary for this work. History and critical theory can aid in deconstructing the legacy of colonial histories and offers an understanding of the processes of power and culture in maintaining practices that appear contradictory to universal human rights. Global minded social work requires an understanding of how the local context shapes experiences of diversity and difference, and this involves reflecting upon personal experiences and perceptions as a social work professional. However, the process also requires a second stage, involving the analysis of the global influences or roles of international stakeholders that may privilege external interests over the needs or interests of the local community. Global influences can also determine implementation of practice ideas that overlook local voices and concerns. Identifying the social consequences of difference and the implications for the quality of life, health, wellbeing and security within people are also necessary to guide action and develop intervention that aspires toward equality.

5 Global Mindedness and Structural Work

Introduction

Social work has been criticised for being preoccupied with state welfare and remedial approaches to social issues, and giving too little attention to social development. Social workers often feel inadequate or frustrated in addressing global issues such as poverty, inequality, and forced migration as they lack awareness of the theories and skills in social development needed to address these issues (Keseke, 1991; Mupedziswa, 1992). Although social workers historically have been involved in social development, it is only recently that these ideas have been explicitly applied to social work practice (Midley and Conoly, 2010). Structural social work involves the development of systems, processes and structures to address the fundamental causes of inequality, address forms of injustice and aim for sustainable social change. As with diversity work, the emphasis is on promoting equality; however, structural social work seeks a restructuring and transformation of society in addition to equity. The goal of structural social work is to alleviate the negative effects of exploitation by the underlying structural conditions and relations that cause oppression (Mullaly, 2007). Social development is a framework that seeks to address injustice at a local community level with the intention of influencing broader institutional and society change.

The involvement of social workers in social development work broadens the scope of social work beyond individual work and is more suited to changing systems and structures at a macro level. For example, in many developing countries social workers are often involved in social develop-ment projects that aim to transform communities. Engagement at the level of policy enables changes at a structural level by outlining visions and strategies to realise this vision. George and Marlowe (2005) also note that radical forms of community work can represent structural social work in action. The activism of women's collective action in the south of India, to pressure the government to take action against sales of alcohol that was incapacitating poor communities (Moore, 1993), is an example of community-based structural social work. In this chapter, we outline various projects and models that can be regarded as structural social work in which social workers are, or can be, involved in.

What Is Structural Work?

Traditional approaches to social work place individuals at the centre of the professional gaze, often resulting in the pathologising or problematisation of the clients' behaviour or circumstances (Moreau, 1979). Structural social work, however, is mainly concerned with addressing social injustices by intervening at the micro and macro dimensions of practice, aiming to achieve structural change. More radical forms of structural work seek a restructuring or transformation of societies and communities. Structural social work has been criticised for being overly idealistic and difficult to practice (George and Marlowe, 2005). However, in a world of growing inequality and oppression, to achieve social justice that is sustainable and embedded in the daily lives organisational structures, structural and policy level work is necessary and in the future will be indispensable.

Structural social work avoids making the dichotomy between the individuals and their situations or contexts by directing attention to the transactions between people and specific social, economic and political situations. Moreau (1979) suggests that the central concern of structural social work is both personal and political power. For example, the high incidence of domestic violence (DV) in Aboriginal communities across Australia has been misleadingly attributed to stereotypes such as Aboriginal woman's passive or dependent behaviour and the patriarchal nature of aboriginal culture. From a structural social work perspective, this type of assessment is lacking and contributes to the further victimisation of indigenous women by focussing on their agency or lack thereof, i.e. that indigenous women have contributed to their own oppression. A structural assessment should explore the relationship between women's personal problems, the dominant ideology (beliefs) and her material conditions (oppression) in the class structure. In this case, what is needed is an analysis of: What makes the experience of DV for indigenous women, as a group, different from other women? How do the dominant ideologies of racism and historical development shape the lives of indigenous people? and What are the ways in which indigenous women exercise their agency? From a structural perspective, the issue is not that an Aboriginal woman has experienced DV and how social workers could support her but to examine this issue in the community and address this at the level of the community and even at the macro level of the nation. From a global mindedness approach, it is essential to understand how social structures contribute to individual behaviour as well as limit their control over their own lives. Australian social workers have challenged simplistic assumptions and asked critical questions as to the how factors of race, gender and power help to explain national trends in DV among indigenous women. A structural analysis of the problem exposes how decades of oppression of indigenous communities have fractured aboriginal community relations. Furthermore, race, economic conditions and dominant ideologies have intersected to create a situation that places Aboriginal women in particularly vulnerable positions and blocks the resources that they should have access to.

Achieving global mindedness in structural social work involves making the connections between government, policy and welfare structures. These structures play a role in the individual experiences that people have. This in turn leads to increased empathy, critical consciousness and empowerment among communities to enable them to envision the changes they want and fight for them (Lundy, 2004). Structural social workers often seek or promote the conditions in which empowerment and emancipation for individuals, communities and society as a whole becomes possible. Structural social work necessarily involves multiple stakeholders, i.e. individuals, family groups, welfare organisations, policy makers and government. Because structural social work is often about promoting the voice and perspective of marginalised local groups in society, it also involves opportunities for active participation. Supporting structural work requires not only respecting democratic movements and decisions but also enabling inclusive, engaging and participative processes so as to ensure where the voices of all groups can be heard.

Power and Structural Work

Structural social work is concerned with processes and ways in which social problems and issues are socially constructed in society. Therefore, an understanding of power and the mechanism through which power is maintained and reproduced is also central. For example, the ways in which the global north dominates the countries of the global south, how white privileged people define the lives of people of colour, how men dominate women, adults speak for children and more generally so-called normal people determine what is deviant; are critical structural questions. Understanding power involves knowledge and theories as to how power functions to limit or marginalise people based on their race, sexual orientation and abilities. This builds upon theories and aims of diversity work.

The tools, interventions and processes involved in structural social work with social justice goals. Therefore, the processes used in structural social work are just as important as the ends. Some examples of structural interventions include forms of advocacy, community work, consciousness raising, and political action, all aimed at systemic change and social development (Wood and Tully, 2006). Structural social work can be aimed at improving structures and lines of communication, creating awareness, integration of services and creation of needs-based services. More radical structural work can involve activism and challenging structures by questioning and challenging the power status quo as well as offering an alternative vision for the future (Popple, 2015: 1). Social workers may engage in subverting repressive rules, challenging oppressive ideologies, opposing transgressions of rights and liberties, and pushing for legislative and policy change (Murray and Hick, 2013). Structural work includes consciousness raising, educational and collective approaches, grounding of issues in terms of material needs, addressing issues of access and distribution of resources, forging alliances between individuals, groups and key stakeholders, and strategic multilevel political action for advancing rights and entitlements (Murray and Hick, 2013). Radical forms of structural social work have become mostly peripheral in most of the work that social workers do. However, in the UK, more attention to social work that focusses on community relations and systems and structures, such as community social work, is undergoing reconsideration. Whether community work will foster structural change and local democracies or simply be used as a resource to link and provide services (Das et al., 2015) remains to be seen. The responsibility for social workers to participate in structural work is reflected in the global definition of social work. In practice the focus has been skewed, making the existing welfare system, services and social policy more responsive to the needs of the oppressed rather than changing the conditions of oppression.

Structural social work has implications even for domestic practice. Professional aims and ethics are increasingly undermined by the influence of managerial and neoliberalist approaches to the welfare profession. These approaches make unrealistic demands in terms of efficiency, productivity and aim to measure outcomes in business terms that are simply not suited to the services that social workers provide. The previous example of the personalisation of welfare services addressed some of these issues. In the global market, social reform and welfare is increasingly commercialised and privatised. Under these conditions, health and welfare services have faced severe financial cuts resulting in increasing numbers of vulnerable people without adequate support systems. Structural social work provides an opportunity to express solidarity and challenge these policies. Developing visions, strategies and services consistent with human rights and social justice ideals falls within the ambit of structural social work.

Policy Reform and Structural Work

One of the most ambitious global policy frameworks aimed at structural reform is the Millennium Development Goals of the United Nations that the International Federation of Social Workers and the International

Association of Schools of Social Work (IASSW) support. The realisation of these goals is dependent on being able to address poverty and inequality at a structural level. There is clearly a need for joined-up, integrated and coherent work across the fields of social, economic and environmental development at global and local levels (Cook and Dugarova, 2014). In mainstream discourses and policy development, issues and goal orientated strategies aimed at societal and structural changes are often missing (Cook and Dugarova, 2015).

Micro or individual social work can also serve as the impetus for structural changes through revisions in policy and law. For example, there are various individual cases that are brought into courts of law which have triggered fundamental changes in the system. For example, recently a homosexual couple won a legal case to have a civil union recognised (BBC, 2018). Before this judgement, only marriage between heterosexual couples was recognised. This case highlighted the structural inequality that legal mandates sometimes reproduce, and led to a change in the law. Similarly, homosexuality was decriminalised in India in 2018 after a group of lawyers contested the laws from colonial times that were in place and criminalised homosexuality.

The following case study critically outlines the role of social policy as the focus of social work intervention. The ability to address social change at the meso and macro levels of practice is reflected in principles of global mindedness. The discussion compares youth policy in the UK with that of Kenya, highlighting how the social, cultural and economic context shapes policy.

Example 5.1

Comparative Youth Policy (Kenya)

Identifying the issues: Internationally, most countries have policies and programs that focus on youth and their development. However, how the term 'youth' is socially constructed and conceptualised varies. In most European countries, youth includes people aged between 15 and 25 years. In the UK, youth often refers to older children or young adults, particularly between the ages of 18 and 19, although people up to 25 years are eligible to receive services aimed for youth. UK policy takes an early prevention approach, with most programs focussing on children rather than youth. In comparison to children's services, the focus on youth remains rather narrow and concerned with social exclusion and youth crime (Biggart, 2008). Youth policy is aimed at reducing disadvantage, supporting education and skills development to promote social and economic integration (Biggart, 2008). In African countries, 'youth', depending on the country, is categorised as people between 15 and 39 years of age

(Gyimah-Brempong and Kimenyi, 2013). Youth is often viewed as an asset and youth policy involves a broader spectrum of programs covering health, economic, social and political issues. For example, in Kenya, youth are defined as people between 15 and 30 years of age and youth policy is focussed on eight strategic areas, namely: Employment; Empowerment and participation; Education and training; Information communication technology; Health; Crime and drugs; Environment; Leisure, Recreation and community service (Youth Policy, 2014).

Critical analysis: The underlying assumption inherent in the policies for youth, both in the UK and in Kenya, is the recognition of youth as a transitional phase in the life course. However, countries tend to give a different emphasis to youth potential, capabilities and status. Youth policies in the UK and in Kenya reflect the demographic, socio-political and economic conditions of their respective countries. In the UK 17.8 per cent of the population are youth (below 15 years of age in 2014) (OECD, 2018) and a relatively high percentage of the population are in their 20s and mid 30s (ONS, 2016). In Kenya, 32 per cent of the population fall under the category of youth and 75 per cent of the population is under 30. The importance of young people to the economy, society and culture also differs significantly between the two countries. In the UK, young people make relatively swift transitions to financial independence and adulthood. Almost half of the youth in the UK achieve higher education and typically enter the labour market at an average age of 21 or 22. The unemployment rate of young people in the UK has been relatively stable at 14 per cent in 2006 (Biggart, 2008) and 13.6 per cent in 2016 (Worldbank.org, 2017). Youth policies centre on the vulnerability and risk associated with youth such as access to employment and education opportunities, and rehabilitation for youth drug and substances abuse or those in contact with the criminal justice system (Biggart, 2008). There is an individualised provision of services through advisors that seek to integrate services and support for youth in need. The UK projects have received mixed reviews as to the effectiveness of social policy and welfare provision in promoting youth integration. While the personalised advisors received positive reviews, the high work load of advisors has received criticism and there remain challenges in appropriately addressing youth with multiple vulnerabilities.

The youth unemployment rate in Kenya as of 2017 was 21.8 per cent (Worldbank.org). Positive youth development and addressing challenges for youth is considered to be related to the achievement of stability and peace in Kenya (discussed in Gyimah-Brempong and Kimenyi, 2013). In Kenya the focus is on generating employment, encouraging entrepreneurship, providing internship opportunities and developing capacity (Kempe, 2012). However, policy evaluations suggest that these policies and programs have not been effective as they have failed to meaningfully enable youth participation and engagement (Kempe, 2012).

Reworking for global mindedness: The consideration of youth policy in the UK and Kenya highlights how the needs of young people are interpreted differently through the lens of social policy. The value of social policy comparisons is not to judge the different approaches, as the needs, resources, infrastructure and historical development of the two societies differ significantly. Rather, a global minded approach is enhanced by the exploration of international social policy and its differing facets – offering opportunities to learn and further develop aspects of policy. It helps to facilitate the questioning of how youth is constructed and young people's developmental needs, and potential and position in society is promoted. Stepping out of our geographical and cultural boundaries fosters dialogue and, ultimately, more creative approaches to addressing social issues.

For example, the development of youth must be linked and integrated with the economic, political, social and environmental systems. A more integrated system that enables an overview and linking of services may help to build trust and encourage youth participation in the Kenyan context. On the other hand, a more inclusive policy aimed at youth development, rather than the focus on excluded youth, may represent a new direction in the UK.

From a global minded approach, international perspectives and examples are aimed at learning and developing practices rather than simply comparing practices between countries. No practices, however, should be simply transferred from one context of another and such knowledge of different policy context does not replace a critical analysis of the local–global relations and a critical understanding of the historical development of a local environment. Policies and developmental strategies that encompass all youth and consider the development of youth as engaged democratic citizens through their engagement in issues such as technology, environment, multiculturalism, and that increasing dialogue across generations, are perhaps good starting points for all countries.

Social Development and Structural Work

Social development and structural work both aim to promote social change and tend to inform each other. Put simply, social development is about putting people at the centre of development. Any commitment to development processes needs to benefit people, particularly the poor or marginalised, at both the micro and macro levels of societies. Social development focusses on the role of formal institutions, legislation and policies in promoting structural change in relation to activities such as the management of aid and welfare projects addressing issues of inequality and injustice including gender discrimination, poverty, education and health of minority groups. However, you should remember that informal social institutions, such as the culture, norms and practices of villages and communities, are also a target of social development at the micro level of social work practice. Social development thus implies change in social institutions and therefore shares common ground with structural social work. Progress toward an inclusive society, for example, implies that individuals treat each other fairly in their daily lives, whether in the family, workplace, or in public office. Social development involves concepts such as social cohesion, social inclusion, empowerment, security and social accountability, which are all related to human rights and participatory governance (Davis, 2004). The indices of social development are used to compare formal and informal social institutions across countries. These indices relate to levels of civil activism, community engagement, interpersonal trust and security, and equality. However, social development has its critics. Increasingly, the interference of international agencies or governments in domestic politics as a way of influencing social structures is viewed with suspicion. The 2016 American elections is one such example where it has been claimed that Russia interfered in the political debates on social media, thereby influencing the presidential elections. International sway over social institutions can be both manifest and latent and may be supported or resisted by local institutions and people. It is thus necessary for global minded social workers to understand the different power structures and relations that go beyond the nation state to ascertain the value of global support and the cost of global interference. An example of how global conditions can both support and hinder democratic local processes is illustrated in the following case studies from India

Example 5.2

Local Activism Versus Global Dominance (India)

Identifying the issues: Indian social work provides many instances as to how practitioners navigate local needs in the face of global pressures.

Case 1: Medha Patkar, a social work graduate from the Tata Institute of Social Services, India, is a famous political activist mobilising villages affected by the proposed damming of tribal land initiated by the Indian Government and financed by the World Bank. With the support of villages, Patkar challenged the project and raised public awareness of the plight of oppressed villages. In so doing, Patkar lobbied for the legal rights of communities across Indian facing similar fates and created a role model internationally. Eventually the World Bank withdrew from the project. In 1996, Patkar went on to found the National Alliance of People's Movements (NAPM), an agglomeration of progressive social bodies opposed to globalisation policies. She became a representative to the World Commission on Dams, the first independent global advisory body on dam-related issues of water, power and alternatives.

Case 2: Within the state of Maharashtra, a policy for women was to be discussed at local levels, involving women participants across various communities and groups as well as women's organisations. During the course of the consultations, it emerged that one of the representative groups was UN funded with a family planning agenda. This caused considerable upset among the other participants as they viewed this as interference from a global organisation with a particular agenda to control women's reproduction rather than representing women. Furthermore, they saw this as undermining the local democratic processes as the UN participants were not necessarily representing local women's agendas.

Critical analysis: Both examples amplify the tensions between local and global priorities in the field of social development in terms of how global agendas penetrate local contexts and structures, and the importance of understanding how global power can be used and resisted. In the first case Patkar presents a prime example of how actions at the local level are often influenced by national and international agencies and how action at the local level can have global impact. In the second example, it becomes clear that the demarcation between local, national and international is not always clear, in particular when international organisations are involved at all levels and have considerably more resources at their disposal than local participants, and can drown out local concerns.

Reworking for global mindedness: There are many inspiring examples of how political and social activism has been used by social workers to challenge global practices by powerful organisations. The interference of international organisations can often lead to further exclusion and lead to additional problems when they are unable to regard local contexts appropriately and truly work with local communities in a participative and collaborative manner. Global influences can occur at different levels that can both encourage or limit local/national activities – but this involvement is multifaceted and has different perspectives. Global support, on the other hand, can also be a supportive force with opportunities of access to resources. Global minded social workers require critical skills to be able to gather and consolidate different perspectives and offer a critical structural analysis. This analysis should then be the basis of their work in the local context.

Questions

- Discuss with a colleague how, and in what respects, an imposition of global standards on local practices may be problematic? In which cases might this be justified?
- Do you know of examples of pressure from external bodies that impact local practice negatively? Or global developments that are resisted at local levels?
- Consider how social workers can use power effectively to address negative global influences? What skills would they need?

History and Structural Work

As outlined in the second chapter, human lives are shaped by the histories, material conditions, ideologies and interactions that mould their cultures. Recognising the importance of history in determining current social issues is another key issue that must be recognised in global minded practice. The historical development of issues and relations between the local and global are also important points to consider in structural work. The following case study on child labour reflects the importance of reworking human rights in light of historical and cultural conditions.

Is it Child Labour? The Case of Columbia: How Policy Influences Practice (Ghana and Bolivia)

Identifying the issues: In many developing countries, children are engaged in work, which defies the UN Charter on the Rights of the Child (1989). Most of these children are employed within the agricultural sector and work alongside their families to supplement their parents' incomes. However, the kind of work that children may engage in and the context varies (Laird, 2012). For example, UN organisations and UNICEF have worked in tandem with the government of Ghana to implement policies and laws to restrict and ban child labour. These measures have been criticised as inadequate and unsuited to the context. Many have argued that the nature and engagement of child labour in many countries cannot be simply categorised as exploitation of children's labour. In some cultural contexts, children's work is considered important not only in the context of labour but as a means of becoming part of society and engaging in social relations, learning and socialisation. Bolivia has been one of the first countries to break ranks with organisations such as UNICEF and has legislated in favour of working children. Bolivia's legislation for the first time includes children's voices and opinions and seeks to protect working children rather than driving working children underground by banning and limiting their chances to work (Liebel, 2014).

Critical analysis: The principles underlying the Ghanaian case and the Bolivian case are both to do with the protection of children. However, while the Ghanaian approach relies on legal mechanisms to restrict children from working and providing them schooling alternatives, the Bolivian approach aims to reconcile children's interests with the practical realities of their lives and offers legislation to protect children from hazardous work. While the two countries' approaches to child labour are seemingly contradictory, they are both orientated to addressing the issues of child labour that harms children, robs them of their dignity and exposes them to exploitation. It is clear that both approaches are informed by different assumptions as to the source of the problem.

Reworking for global mindedness: An historical analysis of social problems and solutions is essential to global mindedness. For example, the concept of when children's work becomes exploitative and harmful is debatable, and is also evolutionary. Children's needs, desires and opportunities for development are not static and respond to the local and global context they are situated in. Policies and practices in terms of addressing issues related to working children need to consider a variety of concerns. While global formulations of problems with regards to children working can help to mobilise resources, solutions to problems that do not take heed of local situations and the broader interrelationship between the global and the local can often be counter-productive. There is also evidence that imposition of well-meaning policies and solutions do not always have positive impacts and result in a waste of time and resources. A global minded approach can open up different possibilities as well as highlighting the different issues that one must consider for context specific intervention.

Questions

- Should social workers in countries where child labour is an historical and cultural reality advocate for the legalisation of child labour?
- Analyse a current social issue by applying an historical and cultural perspective? Does this change your understanding of the issues involved?
- What is the role of structural social work in protecting the rights of children?

Empowerment and Structural Work

Empowerment is a core aim of social work. However, what we mean by empowerment and how much power we share with clients is not always clear. Defined simply, empowerment refers to the capacity of individuals, groups and/or communities to gain control of their circumstances, achieve their own goals and improve the quality of their lives. Empowerment is a personal or collective strength often requiring new resources including capacities, capabilities, choices and a sense of solidarity. The aim of empowerment is to reduce power inequalities in society and, by so doing, unmask the primary structures of oppression. Interventions include facilitating a collective consciousness; fostering activism and encouraging responsibility for feelings and behaviours leading to personal and political change (Carniol, 1992). The following case study of self-help groups demonstrates how empowerment and the sharing of power can facilitate structural change.

Example 5.4

Self-Help Groups (Bangladesh and India)

Identifying the issues: Despite huge amounts of social development aid given by the global north there has been negligible change in the situation of the very poor in countries of the global south. Governments and NGOs have been reluctant to engage in the direct provision of money to the poor preferring to deliver services and aid in kind. This practice continues despite exceptional examples illustrating how giving money directly to the poor can result in individual empowerment and social change. Self-help groups (SHGs), introduced by Mohammed Yunnus in Bangladesh to lift people from poverty through micro credit loans, have developed into a strategic method of working and delivering services that involve people from the grass roots. The basic idea of a SHG is to form a collective group that can regulate itself. SHGs are often used as a collective way to raise money and make finance available for micro credit programs. SHGs are able to finance small projects for people who may be too poor to access money through banks and who may not be able to fulfil the administrative criteria that financial institutions demand. The success and possibilities of the SHGs have enabled development of various programs which have been funded both by the government as well as being funded and supported by NGOs. In India, SHGs play a major role in capacity building and addressing various issues such as health and sanitation, dowries, abuse, child marriages, rain water harvesting, education, building skills, domestic violence, remarriage and so on (Pawar, 2014). SHGs mobilise people to address various socio-economic and cultural issues, and have also been highly successful in mobilising people politically. Women participating in SHGs seem to have more political awareness and are more likely to become members of elected local governing bodies. SHGs thus not only support individuals, but also are increasingly becoming an alternative source and mode of service delivery. For example, in some areas, local women's SHGs groups are contracted to provide mid-day meals for children in local schools.

Critical analysis: SHGs can help people who are poor to access money locally without being trapped by loan sharks, giving people opportunities to develop projects using the skills they possess. Yet, the opportunities provided by SHGs and to what extent they have an impact depend on local people and cultures. Thus, a concept such as SHGs readily becomes a strategy for social development at the micro level in terms of supporting individuals and groups. This concept, however, can bring about positive gains at the meso level through building community links and integrating excluded people in the community. Nevertheless, SHGs can be very limited in their capacity for empowerment and change when this becomes embedded within existing power structures rather than changing them. Thus, there can be little empowerment of women, when women's gains through their participation in SHGs become absorbed into patriarchal relations within their families and communities instead of transforming patriarchal relations.

Reworking for global mindedness: Social entrepreneurial interventions, such as SHGs, demonstrate the importance of creativity, or looking beyond the box. At the grass-roots level, SHGs can facilitate people to find their own solutions to complex problems, thereby creating opportunities for structural reform. Social worker skills that become necessary in such projects include: knowledge and skills for community building, empathy, the ability to motivate people and seek participation, as well as the knowledge and skills to link people with available services and opportunities. Action research skills, such as participatory research, and the ability to record and communicate outcomes across levels is also important, particularly to lobby for issues or promote best practices (Selener, 1997). Nevertheless, no intervention or strategy should be taken at face value but need to be evaluated and considered in view of the results produced in a particular context.

Questions

- Why do you think governments and NGOs are reluctant to give money to the poor?
- What are the processes involved that bring about individual and social change as outlined in the example? What are some of the risks involved?
- How does this understanding influence creative ways to work with clients in your domestic practice? Do you see opportunities for group work, such as self-help groups, in your practice?

Intergenerational Relations and Structural Work

Solidarity and conflict within intergenerational relations may also be considered as the focus of structural work. Immigration, women's participation in labour and the breakdown of nuclear families have led to complex familial structures, where communication, care and contact are constantly negotiated by family members, often across large geographical distances. Demographic changes resulting in increased life expectancy and lowered fertility has resulted in people living longer and in more complex family structures. For example, grandparents and great grandparents have longer life expectancies but their care often occurs outside of the family unit and communication with grandchildren often crosses national borders. With increasing reductions in available governmental resources, it is especially important to understand the changing nature of multigenerational family structures, the impact on individual wellbeing and the effectiveness of the informal and formal supports available. Families that have more generations living together are a source of additional sources of support, wisdom and resources. However, the negative consequences of this phenomenon, such as intergenerational conflict and competition for resources, could potentially emerge (Antonucci, 2007). Multigenerational support systems represent examples of informal social structures which global minded social workers must be aware of in their practice. There is a need to design future support programs with these challenges in mind. The following case example draws out the need for structural and community reform to better integrate older people into families and societies.

Example 5.5

Older Women's Contribution to Crafting Communities (Australia)

Identifying the issues: It is difficult to escape the pessimistic messages about the 'burden' of Australia's ageing population (Maidment and Macfarlane, 2011). Public policy planning reports and academic commentary abound with references to the critical fiscal, health and social challenges presented by this population cohort (Borowski, 2007). Newspaper headlines often highlight that the ageing population is a time bomb set to destroy the prospects of the younger generation, reinforcing messages of gloom and doom about growing tensions and conflict and competitions over resources between the younger and older generations. Ageing in the global north is undoubtedly a complex and diverse personal experience and a challenging social issue. Of course, ageing in the global south is just as complex given the sheer number of people over the age of 65 in those countries. Globally, the positionality of older people in society is changing and in some cases in negative ways that diminish their status and rights.

Social workers have considered alternative discourses that challenge dominant stereotypes of older people as merely burdens on society. Counter discourses are needed that solidly reflect the principles of community development, and challenge stereotypical thinking about older women as dependent, isolated and unproductive. Maidment and Macfarlane (2011) present one such counter narrative of a resilient and committed group of older women quietly and steadily contributing to community fundraising, building social networks and providing learning opportunities to each other in diverse ways. While none of the older women concerned were trained in any form of community work, their participation led to further creation of social capital, fostering of life-long learning through craft work, fund raising, fostering social support network activities and wellbeing. This was a positive example that demonstrated how sustained community development can lead to transformative social relations and political activity (Maidment and Macfarlane, 2008). The women's craft groups provide an excellent example of local people being involved in locally sustainable enterprises: the groups produced little pollution, engaged in recycling of materials such as fabrics and patterns, and were able to survive and grow in ways that were not harmful to the environment. Similarly, in Germany, multigenerational activities are common, where local community or church groups offer open spaces and activities for people across generations to participate in. This can be as simple as opening a community space once a week for subsidised coffee and cake, or bigger housing projects where families with children, older people, people with disabilities and young people can live together.

Critical analysis: What then can we learn from community-based examples of structural work? The importance of informal local networks has been increasingly recognised in the social policies of 'western' nations (Trevithick, 2005: 226). At the same time, Trevithick (2005) cautions that informal social supports, provided mostly by the women (Ife, 2002: 12) in the family, should not be seen as a replacements for State obligations to provide needed services. Ife (2002: 2) reminds us that community-based supports and community work in general 'must always be seen within the context of the crisis of the welfare state'.

Reworking for global mindedness: Global minded social workers need to be critically reflective around the empowering or disempowering nature of care. Some marginalised groups may not be in a space to organise themselves to 'gain control over resources and issues which face them' (Payne, 2005: 221). Community and structurally minded social workers may have a role in facilitating such groups to engage in community action and group involvement, assisting individuals to connect, advocate for resources and provide consultation or skilled community members to deal creatively with issues they have identified as important (Ife, 2002: 93). Ife has highlighted the use of sustainable local resources, the value of existing local skills and processes as important attitudes and practices for community minded social workers. Social workers should consider ways in which they might both support these informal group networks, while acknowledging the significant contribution such endeavours can make in the lives and wellbeing of individual people. Small group work activities are empowering, democratic, participative and humanistic and may indirectly impact on structural change in relation to oppressive social conditions. Social workers clearly need to be aware of how dominant discourses serve to both enable and oppress, and acknowledge inequality among older people, and how this plays out in specific contexts. The principle of diversity is crucial to community work and social development, the capacity of systems, groups, informal networks, and communities to 'evolve to meet the needs of particular circumstances', to encourage and embrace a range of responses, forms and levels of participation, and to allow the possibility of different ways of doing things (Ife, 2002: 43–44). The principle of diversity applies to differences within communities, as well as between communities. As social workers, we need to remain mindful that one group of older people, may be quite different to another, and within each group (Ife, 2002). Social workers can help find ways to validate and celebrate diversity, acknowledging the rights of potentially marginalised and invisible people – such as older women – to define their needs, ways of meeting those needs and providing support to enable truly successful (or perhaps more appropriately 'meaningful') lives. In this example we have attempted to highlight the need for critical analysis and reflection as social workers, on discourses of ageing, participation and gender role expectations.

Questions

- How are issues of older age discussed in global and local contexts?
- What international theories of structural social work could inform practice with marginalised individuals and families?
- Give examples of how community work or social development may challenge oppressive relationships and structures?

Summary

It is through a structural perspective that the sheer scope and power of globalisation becomes visible to individual social workers. While the structural perspective is sometimes difficult to grasp and engage with, the opportunities for transformative social work are greater. In this chapter, we have provided examples that have highlighted the need to address social injustices by intervening at the meso and macro levels of practice simultaneously. This chapter also reiterates that critically working across different levels requires an understanding of power, history and the impact of informal and formal structures on the lives of people. Furthermore, as we will uncover in the next chapter, global issues such as climate, fair economics and migration also demand strategies at the global structural level. The inter-relationship between protection, diversity and structural work is further explored by the concept of sustainability.

6 Global Mindedness and Sustainability Work

Introduction

Environmental sustainability is a global concern as the available resources cannot continue to sustain growing human populations at the rate of consumption that humans have become accustomed to. It can be argued that the road to an environmentally sustainable future requires an interdisciplinary response that engages both the social and physical sciences (Schmitz et al., 2012). In social work, there are three types of sustainability that are generally considered: social, economic and environmental (Mary, 2008). Social workers are familiar with social sustainability, which recognises that individual health and wellbeing, nutrition, shelter, education and cultural needs must be met (Brennan, 2010; Mary, 2008). Within the current IFSW Global Agenda for Social Work and Social Development (2012), one of the main themes refers to 'working toward environmental and community sustainability'. Students are introduced to the concept of the person-in-environment paradigm. This paradigm is closely aligned to the concept of environmental sustainability as the environment very much shapes the experiences of a person, and without supportive environments, enhancing human quality of life is not possible. While often only the social and emotional environments are considered as important, the physical environment plays a significant role in determining health outcomes for individuals and communities. Historically, social work education has been slow to engage with the environmental issues of our times. This is, however, changing, partly because of the influence of the global agenda. Sustainability work involves research and social work practice concerned with sustainable lifestyles, sustainable consumption of resources, environmental degradation, industrial pollution and climate change, as these have a direct impact on the quality of life of people and communities.

What Is Sustainability Work?

The concept of environmental sustainability is now more generally referred to as sustainability, as it relates not only to the biological or physical environment, but the built, social and political environment as well. For example, environmental issues are often a direct cause of natural disasters, migration, war and conflicts arising from competition over scarce natural resources such as water, land (territory) and clean air. Sustainability in the context of social work refers to concerns as to the preservation of biodiversity as part of human survival, social sustainability, and social and environmental justice (Schmitz et al., 2012).

Environmental, green or sustainable social work is embedded in a tradition of social justice and offers transformative opportunities to expand our understanding of individuals in their environments. Perhaps Dominelli's (2012) definition of green social work best captures our notion of sustainability work from a global mindedness approach. She refers to practice that intervenes to protect the environment and enhance people's wellbeing by integrating the interdependencies between people and their socio-cultural economic and physical environments, and among peoples within an egalitarian framework that address prevailing structural inequalities and unequal distribution of power and resources. People living in poverty enjoy fewer environmental rights, live in degraded social and physical environments and are disproportionately subject to industrial pollution and natural disasters. For example, in 2017, many people died in a huge fire that engulfed Grenfell Tower, a west London social housing tower block. It was claimed that the cost cuts made on the outside cladding material used for the refurbishment of the building may have contributed to the fire and consequently the loss of so many lives. The Grenfell action group had warned that the building was a fire risk before and after the refurbishment. Subsequently, the government has tested over 600 similar buildings in the country and so far at least 190 structures, designed for the economically disadvantaged, have failed to meet adequate standards of safety (BBC, 2017). While much is made of the increasing number of ghettos, slums and shantytowns in the global south, industrialisation and urbanisation in the both the global south as well as the global north contribute to declining health, wellbeing and quality of life of the poor and marginalised.

Globalised capital and trade has resulted in decisions that have been made by transnational organisations and conglomerates affecting local people's environments . In turn this makes it increasingly difficult to hold anyone accountable or responsible under national laws for poor practices resulting in disasters and human suffering. Furthermore, the conditions of industrialisation and post-industrialisation have a detrimental effect on physical and mental health leading to the break up of traditional family systems and forms, stress, higher morbidity, respiratory diseases, loss of livelihoods, social isolation and stigma. For example, internal migration from rural to urban areas fuelled by unregulated urbanisation often leads to inequitable hardship for workers and their families. The example of China's left behind children illustrates how parents in rural areas are forced, due to poverty, to migrate to larger cities for employment. As a consequence the children are left in the care of grandparents in regional areas. Becoming a left behind child may have an indirect and negative influence on the child's wellbeing, health and educational opportunities. Many countries have examples of where economic development has resulted in one or both parents in working class families living separately from their children or older family members due to work opportunities elsewhere. One should not be too quick to judge the rationale behind parents' decisions to be separated from their children and older family members. These personal decisions are ultimately forced by national and international politics and economics and peoples' desire to seek a better life for their families. In turn, rural–urban migration has a direct impact on the environment and quality of life for people in countries of the global south and the global north. In Australia, for example, changes in large scale mechanised agricultural practices have resulted in environmental issues, such as soil degradation, and the depletion of underground water supplies. Fewer employment opportunities for agricultural workers have contributed to the demise of once vibrant regional agricultural towns and the social experiences and culture associated with this traditional way of life. The plight of left behind children in China and the demise of rural towns in Australia are now concerns for those who have an interest in sustainability work.

Humans have accelerated the process of climate change to a point where it is now the largest social issue of our time (Orr, 2011). As humans, we constitute a small part in the larger ecosystem; however, we have an immense capacity to both destroy the environment as we attempt to satisfy our needs and want as well as to scale back the environmental degradation, ensuring sustainability (Stocker and Kennedy, 2009). The main reason for much of the degradation of the physical environment is the need of the powerful to maintain their political, cultural and economic privileges (Faux, 2006; Levy and Vaillancourt, 2011). In many cases the destruction of the physical environment is an outcome of unrestrained or unregulated capitalism where natural resources are commodified, as large, powerful corporations search for cheap labour and locations free from pollution regulation (Hoff and Polack, 1993; Patel and Moore, 2017). Within contemporary capitalist systems, greed trumps all and neither human nor environmental wellbeing is protected. Patel and Moore (2017) argue that this exploitation of the environment is grounded in enlightenment philosophies where man has sought to control nature.

Global advances in technology have the capacity to liberate and empower people, i.e. use of health monitoring for people who have a disability or are frail or elderly, and free access to education and information. However, the increasing inequality of access to such technology has resulted in new forms of social injustice. For example, the use of science for genetic modification of grains as well as genetically modified production of milk and meat have long reaching implications for the environment in terms of soil and plant diversity as well as on the quality of ecosystems and human life. The impact of technology has resulted in the growing social exclusion of some groups of people, such as older people, who do not find technology user-friendly, and people in the global south who cannot afford the hardware and software required to secure access to the World Wide Web. The use and availability of technology is clearly complex and technology, by itself, cannot offer a panacea to all issues of sustainability and environmental damage.

Sustainability work has been theorised from several perspectives: ecosystems, structural or critical theory and human rights. This type of work involves highly political and often change-orientated interventions, such as advocacy, mobilisation and organisation of people and communities, as well as lobbying for policy reform.

Environment and Sustainability Work

Coates (2003), who sees social injustice in the 'quest for economic growth and profit', lists several immediate environmental concerns that are simultaneously exploitive to people and the environment. Deforestation has deprived indigenous people of their homeland. The toxic pollution of natural environments results in increased disease counts and mortality rates in communities. Overfishing has depleted both the oceans and the livelihood of people dependent on the industry. Issues of access and social justice are very much linked to environmental issues (Philip and Reisch, 2015).

Environmental racism is rampant, demonstrated by industries dumping waste in poor neighbourhoods, countries and peripheral locations. The trade in garbage, where technological waste is dumped in developing countries for processing, is also an example of the unequal impact of environmental issues. People who overconsume are often not the ones who directly suffer the consequences of their consumption. Environmental illnesses have dramatically increased in recent years; for example, higher rates of asthma in urban children. As Coates (2003) states 'When the Earth has been senselessly exploited and polluted, social injustice has been a result' (p. 24). The global mining industry is one of the main sources of environment pollution and the exploitation of rural communities illustrated in the example below.

Example 6.1

Unequal Consequences of Environmental Exploitation (Finland, India)

Identifying the issues: Mineral and energy resource mining is a global enterprise monopolised by large international companies, which have little or no moral accountability to any nation. Furthermore, these environmental exploitations often result in disastrous consequences for the physical and human environment. Examples of the uneasy tensions between economic development and concerns as to the preservation of pristine environments and indigenous cultures and lifestyles are numerous; for example, fracking in the rural communities of the west coast of Ireland, uranium mining on the Aboriginal tribal lands of Australia, gas fields on the traditional lands of North American Indians.

Critical analysis: Mining exploration is usually centred on peripheral locations. Ranta-Trykkö (2014) explores these themes through a unique comparison of the impact of mining in northwest Finland and in the eastern state of Odisha, India. While dissimilar in many respects, both countries have a history of colonisation and oppression and discrimination with regards to indigenous peoples. Both countries have significant sites for large mining industries. Both have experienced the adverse effects of the mining processes, i.e. extraction, and longer lasting effects – pollution of waste products, acid drainage – not to the mention the depletion of resources for future generations. Mining is known to be harmful to indigenous populations (i.e. the Sami peoples in northern Finland, tribal communities in India) and removes their customary rights to land and natural resources. This example highlights the material dependence of the first world on the finite resources of the most obscure peripheries or zones of invisibility (Brennan, 2006). The nature of this exploitation of vulnerable communities also represents a form of colonisation. It disfigures landscapes and denies access to the inhabitants of the mined area to what was once familiar or sacred. Despite an awareness of continual resource depletion, it appears that nothing will change as long as the dominant agenda for economic growth persists.

Reworking for global mindedness: This example demonstrates the need for environmentally conscious practice (i.e. skills, interventions), theory and research (Brennan, 2006) to make the impact of natural resource depletion more visible to those that overconsume and to question our assumption that natural resources are something to be consumed and exploited.

The arguments used to justify environmental exploitation almost always involve the competition of rights between minority and indigenous peoples, and the mainstream or elite majorities. However, promoting awareness of the environment as a living ecosystem helps to deflect inequality and conflict by reframing the problem as on that is shared. The consequences of environment damage impact everyone, irrespective of the status of particular groups of people. In addition, even if the direct impact of environmental damage at first seems to affect only a few people, the indirect and long-term effects of this damage affects all across the globe.

It becomes important, as social workers, to not only reframe these issues as being of concern to all, but also to proactively change ideas and lifestyles that support sustainability. No single individual and no single practice can remedy our unsustainable lifestyles. However, large-scale small changes do have impact. There remains huge scope to learn different ways of thinking about the environment and different ways of sustaining ecosystems from traditional and indigenous communities.

Questions

- Why do you think social workers have been largely inactive in the field of environmental sustainability?
- What is the nexus between environmental and community sustainability?
- Can you give examples where social workers have worked with communities to counteract the impact of environmental exploitation on traditional lifestyles and human wellbeing? What skills and knowledge did they employ in their efforts?

Social Development and Sustainability Work

Sustainability issues are closely linked to social development as well as structural work. Natural disasters have often been the result of environmental degradation and may result in further damage to the physical and social environment. Building resilience and sustainable structures and communities after a disaster or crisis is therefore the aim of aid or social development work. In the wake of various disasters around the world (i.e. cyclones in Bangladesh and India, tsunamis in the Philippines, earthquakes in Nepal and Japan, cyclones in the USA, bushfires in Australia), global society has worked in tandem with local actors to address the needs of those who are displaced and vulnerable. Global responses have included international efforts to raise funds as well as the involvement of international governments to provide aid and logistical support. Nevertheless, local actors remain key in responding immediately, quickly and at the grassroots level. Cooperation in response to disasters provides many examples as to how local and global efforts can work in tandem with similar visions without replication and waste of resources and time.

Karger et al. (2012) outline how NGOs have played a key response role in the bushfires in Australia, and with Hurricane Katrina as well as in the numerous disasters that have hit India. When local actors, through voluntary services as well as local NGOs, are able to organise well and link seamlessly with national and international support, the outcomes for vulnerable people are necessarily better. Local actors and NGOs can mobilise the grass roots quickly and effectively, and can make the most of the logistical and material support from external bodies. Within this context, it becomes necessary for communities and people to be prepared and trained to manage disasters and social workers can play a key role in such capacity building. Social workers can also play an important role in responding to crises by helping to organise and manage rescue and rehabilitation efforts. Social worker skills can also be very helpful in helping to organise communities to respond to disaster and to rebuild. Furthermore, social workers can engage in community groups, as well as with individual-orientated work, in supporting people to deal with trauma and in the use of therapeutic services.

However, the context of disasters and global aid also provides many examples of difficulties arising when global actors take charge and ignore local sentiments and needs. In the following case study we discuss an example of famine as an environmental disaster and issues with global responses.

Example 6.2

Failed or Faulty Aid? (Kenya)

Identifying the issues: In 2006, New Zealand offered dog food as assistance against starvation to populations in northern Kenya. During the famine, Kenya was offered 42 tons of powdered dog food (Schwabe, 2006). The Kenyan government rejected this offer in spite of assurances from the food manufacturer that the food would be supplemented with appropriate vitamins, was actually quite nutritious and tasty, and the powder could be easily mixed with water to create a ready breakfast. The offer deeply hurt the dignity of Kenyan people, who expected their starving children to at least be treated with the humanity they deserved.

Critical analysis: Issues of inequality become clearly visible at the global level. Most are aware of southern countries, which are often labelled as 'developing countries', and northern countries are often considered as 'developed countries'. It is ironic that the countries with the most natural resources are the 'developing countries' but that most of the wealth in the world is concentrated in 'northern' countries. Historically, it is evident that various processes of exploitation, colonisation and capitalism have led to particular socio-economic and political dynamics resulting in this inequality between northern and southern countries. After the gradual dismantling of colonialism, at least in terms of direct rule, with a view to addressing these inequalities, enabling development and supporting human rights, various strategies have been developed to support southern countries to create systems of self-reliance and independence. Aid, developmental funds, loans, transfer of expertise and other benevolent schemes are the primary strategies used by northern countries to assist southern countries in their development. However, such aid, in turn, often cheapens lives in developing countries and undermines empowerment principles as in this example.

Critical analysis: It is clear from this example, that even in disaster work, local people and their concerns need to be considered; people must be treated with dignity and have the opportunity to determine their destinies. Often local people are best suited to work with natural resources and to develop plans that are sustainable. However, as this example highlights, aid from northern countries often cheapens the lives, dignities and resources of local persons in offering aid or services that would be questionable in their own countries. This is evident and visible across various dimensions. For example, it is common for Germans to teach in English-speaking colonies, where the populations speak English. However, English speakers from these countries are hardly ever recognised as native English speakers to teach English in Germany. Furthermore, the issue of aid has become increasingly problematic as it maintains the status quo of helper versus those who are to be helped. There is little change in terms of structures that lead to the conditions of exploitation, in which northern countries are often directly and indirectly implicit. In addition, northern countries often fail to clearly take responsibility for the impact that colonisation and capitalism has had from which they have benefitted – but at the cost of environments, local populations and even by undermining local democracies (Patel and Moore, 2017).

Reworking for global mindedness: The politics of development has often meant that countries in the global north support development in countries of the global south. However, there is an urgent need to reassess and rework these relationships to enable true development and self-reliance. Poverty in the global south is not coincidental, but a result of a series of mechanisms that consistently diminishes and cheapens the labour, work, environments and outputs in southern countries. Unless these mechanisms are addressed, issues of famine, environmental disasters and interconnected with that civil unrest and migration, will continue to shape developing countries. It is the responsibility of, and is in the interest of, northern countries to address these issues and the power imbalances if actual development is to be achieved. However, the political will, as well as the vision of a global humanity that prioritises this, has often been lacking. Indeed, it is difficult to address these unequal power relationships that sustain underdevelopment because the rich benefit from this cheapening of labour, resources and environments. As global minded social workers then, it becomes vital to address these issues at the structural levels of policy. It also becomes important to interconnect the various ways in which economics, labour, environments and money, among various other factors, play a role in determining the quality of people's lives. Finally, it is critical that social workers not take mental short-cuts and focus their attention to managing need and disaster but also make efforts to address causal factors across all levels.

Questions
- Would you be willing to accept dog food for your family members, if they were in dire need?
- What are the processes that can transform humanitarian aid into other forms of oppression and dehumanisation?
- How would you in your everyday practice contribute to the self-reliance of people and address issues of sustainability of people's lifestyles?

While natural disasters may initially affect everyone equally, people with more resources are better equipped to access the social and financial resources needed to escape the worst effects of disasters as well as to rebuild their lives. Similarly, it is often seen that richer communities receive better and more support in the aftermath of disasters than poorer communities. This was visible in the aftermath of Hurricane Katrina in the gulf coast of USA in 2005 which drastically affected over 1 million people. However, in the aftermath of the crisis, there was sharp criticism in terms of how ill prepared governance structures were to deal with the crisis, and in particular the unequal treatment of poorer black communities, such as those in New Orleans.

The issue of inequality of access to support and relief is also visible on a global level where one can see the ways in which disaster victims in more developed countries such as Australia are supported in comparison to disaster victims in Bangladesh. The causes of natural disasters are often global; however, the local impacts of such disasters are uneven. Thus, while Bangladesh, as an economically poor country, has a minimal contribution to climate change as compared to western industrialised nations, on account of its particular location and financial vulnerability, Bangladeshi people disproportionately suffer the consequences of climate change.

In recent years, the role and ethical behaviour of international non-government aid relief organisations have been criticised for adopting top down approaches to aid, insensitivity to cultural practices and failure to meet goals as illustrated in the following case study.

Example 6.3

Experience of Community Development (Mozambique)

(Special thanks to Cuinhane 2006, for providing this example.)

Identifying the issues: Upon its independence in 1975, Mozambique would not allow the creation of local associations or the interventions of international humanitarian organisation due to the then socialist regime. In 1990, the new National Constitution allowed everybody to create associations at all levels (political, social economic and cultural areas) and opened the way for international organisations (INGOs) to deliver aid and to help refugees and people in need. It was in this context that community development gained major importance in Mozambique. In 2006 an international organisation was established in Mozambique with the aim to implement 'Child Centred Community Development in rural districts of Inhambane province'. The approach of the project was a strategy consisting of a rights-based approach where children, families and communities are active and leading participants in their own development. This means that before any intervention, an assessment of community realities, such as the main social problems and concerns of the children and households, was to take place. It is on the basis of this assessment that projects were to be designed and then implemented. The implementation was to take community participation into account.

After the organisation was established in the community and had explained its objectives to local stakeholders and communities, it undertook a social research and community assessment of the social and economic status of children (nutrition, civil registration, education, etc.) and the community (type of households, means of subsistence, water and sanitation, health, etc.). The method used in both research and community assessment was a participatory rural appraisal (PRA) and participatory learning action and involved national social workers and social researchers. Information about education, sanitation and the livelihoods of the community was reported. According to the data gathered, the district had extreme poverty, malnutrition, lack of access to education, lack of school materials, high rates of pupils giving up in primary schools, starvation, bad sanitary conditions, lack of knowledge of how to use local resources to enhance household livelihoods, and lack of access to birth registration. The next stage involved prioritising the needs of the community in education and sanitation. Based on the data collected in the community, the first project was designed to intervene in the area of education. However, the community and school council were not involved in the project design. The objective of the project was to retain pupils at primary school and motivate children to learn agricultural activities on a small farm that each school had been developing as part of economic learning activities. The project consisted of distribution of materials to schools, such as exercise books, rulers, pens, pencils, seeds, cutlasses and hoes.

Although the community and school councils said that they were happy about the aid they had received, the evaluation undertaken after the implementation of the project revealed that children were not inspired to continue school and the drop-out rates from school remained high. The reasons linked to these attitudes were the long distance that children had to walk on foot from home to school, lack of sustainable basic needs such as food, clothes and shelter, early marriage and involvement of the children in the household activities, live-stock care and agriculture. Most of the time, the decision of when and whose child should go to school was made by the head of the family. This meant that most children gave up school because their parent helped them to do so. Parents always evaluated their situation according to their everyday lives, and most children were obliged to help their parents to fetch water, take care of livestock and agriculture. These activities were priority for the families because they enabled them to solve their immediate problem: subsistence.

Critical analysis: The community development project described above reveals that it is important to access communities' concerns before implementing any project. Although the approach used was based on people-centred development and accessed the community situation, it had a limited impact on the children. This was due to two main problems: the first is related to lack of knowledge of people's culture (social norms, values, traditional knowledge and views regarding development of children) and the social organisation of the community (social division of activities, role of each member of the family, including male and female children). The social research undertaken did not probe into cultural issues and this influenced the impact of the project. The second problem was related to lack of people's participation in the project design. This led the project to focus on a social problem that was important to the INGO, but was not priority for the community. Instead, the priority of the community was the satisfaction of their everyday needs.

Reworking for global mindedness: In this case study, it is clear that collecting research data from a community without understanding their lives and their culture as a whole does not necessarily work. Whatever experience we have personally on development issues, we should remember that we are never expert enough to know everything there is to know about a community that we have met for the first time. We should also learn that before the implementation of any project we should involve the target group during project design and we should ensure that we are addressing the actual needs of the targeted people. In many international aid organisations, due to funding constraints, projects methods, aims and goals are often determined according to global standards that ignore local norms. This makes the success of such projects in local contexts difficult. Community work necessarily involves understanding local communities and negotiating and finding common ground between global aims and local frameworks.

Questions

- To what extent are recipients of aid or social services involved in the identification of their own needs and the design of projects to address their needs?
- Consider the reasons why social development or community-based projects are often challenging and fail to meet aims?
- How could social development programs be evaluated in relation to sustainability?

Transnationalism and Sustainability Work

Transnationalism is a social phenomenon that refers to the interconnectivity between people as they cross borders as the result of migration, employment and telecommunication. Increasingly, people are becoming involved in transnational networks of social relationships, exchange and participation that span different countries and shape their sense of identity as individuals and groups (Vertovec, 2001). Social workers often work with such people and in contexts where crossing borders is part of the day-to-day experience.

Issues of sustainability are linked to local democracies, as local people know best how to use, as well as preserve, their resources; primarily because their lives often depend on it. Yet sustainability is also concerned with global issues. As illustrated in the previous example, global mechanisms play a significant role in the ways that capitalism and power relations are produced and reproduced. Global mindedness requires global commitment but also local support and involvement. Bringing the interests of various global and local actors together is a difficult task. As is evident in the negotiations to limit global warming, there are global and local actors that can support, but also hinder, positive development. It is also clear that political commitment for global issues is necessary to break cycles of dependence and exploitation. This requires international, multinational and transnational engagement where resources are diverted to address issues that affect everyone and to acknowledge the human rights of all humans, irrespective of their nationality. Failure to recognise human rights and provide access for all does not just result in disadvantage for particular groups of people but will extend to the further deterioration of the planet and loss of quality of life on a worldwide scale. We believe, however, that working across and beyond nation states is both necessary and possible.

Our final case study draws on the issues of recent migration and refugees in Europe and why only a transnational, global minded response can address the causes and effects of this migration.

Example 6.4

Middle Eastern and African Migration and Refugees (European countries)

Identifying the issues: In 2015, Europe faced unprecedented numbers of migrants and refugees arriving at its borders. These were people escaping civil war, famine, community violence and/or a future without any prospects in their home countries (Afghanistan, Iran, Iraq, Somalia, Sudan, Syria). These were all people risking their lives to try to come to Europe with dreams of a better future, a better life, in European countries, that are rich, resourceful and where there is high demand for labour. One could argue that this could almost be a win-win situation. However, the reception of these migrants and refugees was not always welcoming. While Germany and Sweden were more willing to accept refugees, other European countries such as Hungary were less willing and closed their borders to asylum seekers. Nevertheless, a couple of years later, even the goodwill shown by countries such as Italy, Greece, Germany and Finland dissolved in response to increasing right-wing nationalism, demands to close the borders and increasing fears of terrorism, populism and radicalisation, and the cultural and economic implications associated with refugee immigration. Since 2015, European governments have introduced various strategies to limit the arrival of asylum seekers and refugees – from stricter border controls, deportations, restrictions on family reunion and pacts with neighbouring transit countries to block passageways into Europe. More recently, the traditional transit countries such as Italy and Greece have introduced tighter measures to control their borders and claimed that mainland European countries have not supported their humanitarian efforts. It remains to be seen what impact these strategies will have on migration as the reasons for migration and refuge seeking from both the middle east and Africa still exist. The implementation of barriers have had the unintended consequence of creating additional vulnerabilities and risks for men, women and children seeking to escape or searching for better lives, i.e. the lucrative trade in human tracking resulting in the abuse and the death of asylum seekers using these illegal services.

Critical analysis: It is clear that desperate conditions and lack of access to information and opportunities drives extremely vulnerable people to risk their lives to arrive in Europe. Such people suffer and face risks at every step of their journey: in their home countries where they are seeking escape from hardship and difficult conditions, during transit where they are again abused and exploited and very often even in European countries, where they are exploited as cheap labour or as sex slaves, by traffickers and trafficking networks. This exploitation is possible due to the high demand for cheap labour and sexual services in European countries. It is also clear that such cheap labour, while profitable for businesses places domestic workers at risk. However, strengthening borders does little to address the situation in any part of the migrants'/refugees' journeys and instead makes trafficking profitable.

Reworking for global mindedness: It can be argued that the issue of forced migration requires increased transnational collaboration and responses for a sustainable solution. At the heart of the problem is the devaluation of the lives of some people and the cheapening of their labour. Indeed, cheap labour would not be an issue if the migrants' labour was not so cheap or if labour in Europe was equally cheap. For the migrants' labour to be equally valuable, their environments, their lives, available opportunities and access to these opportunities needs to match realistic expectations that can support positive human rights. This again requires positive structural work in migrant home countries and a reworking of the relationships between Europe and the migrants' home countries. As highlighted in the previous example, throwing global aid at projects that are unsuited to local cultures is not sustainable. There is clearly a need for global funding to be better planned and utilised. Global minded social workers can play a critical role in these functions. As long as the quality of migrants' lives remains precarious, there is little chance of successfully controlling migration through brute force, such as the construction of barriers and the policing of borders.

Questions

- In what ways can countries collaborate to ensure a more humane response to the global issue of forced migration?

- How can migrants, i.e. refugees, asylum seekers, be better prepared to make the choice to leave their own country?
- What are the barriers and opportunities for transnational practice in your work?

Summary

Environmental and community sustainability is arguably the most pressing global issue of the decade and therefore central to our notion of global mindedness. Current and future social issues should be analysed from a more holistic perspective of social, political and environmental sustainability. Sustainability work embraces a fundamental commitment to social justice, the value of human beings and the environment and is closely linked to structural work and social development. Social workers should be prepared to rethink and reframe issues relating to social justice and environmental rights to counteract conservative as well as populist and nationalistic attitudes. Participatory strategies, community-focussed action and collective advocacy are key approaches in promoting sustainable solutions to increasingly globalised problems.

7 Global Mindedness in Practice

Introduction

In the previous chapters, the concept of global mindedness has been explored, encouraging students and practitioners to consciously locate their praxis at the intersection between the local and the global. A re-examination of traditional roles and boundaries in social work has been encouraged so as to promote the profession's future relevancy in a globalised world. We have described the context of social work and the impact of globalisation, technology, post-industrialisation and colonialisation in shaping a more globally aware approach to professional practice. Relevant values, theories, approaches and skills were outlined for application in both domestic transnational, and international practice. The practice of global mindedness was explored using different categorisations, i.e. protection, equality, structural and environmental work. Examining case studies from different regions of the world not only facilitated an analysis of different traditions in social work but also offered new insights as to the causes of social phenomena based on alternative cultural perspectives. The case studies also highlighted that issues of protection, diversity, structural contexts and sustainability issues very much intersect and are inter-related. Global mindedness in international social work is therefore about pushing the boundaries and borders of professional practice in order to achieve more futuristic and transformative practice.

Pushing Boundaries

Global mindedness in social work involves a questioning of boundaries of all kinds. Geographical and political borders should not confine practice. In contemporary societies, the notion of nation states is fundamental to our ways of thinking of, and perceiving, the world (Billig, 1995). For example, transnational social work and social work without borders falls within the scope of international social work. To achieve global mindedness, an ability to distance oneself from the idea of nation states is important if one is to recognise the common humanity of all people. This is not to say that one should not have pride in one's own heritage and culture but rather to be able to see how one's identity is not only linked with nation but is linked globally. Critical reflection is useful to identify barriers and self-defences that detract us from this perspective. For example, the phenomenon of forced immigration highlights the need for social workers to communicate and collaborate across national borders, i.e. refugee countries of origin, transit countries and host countries. Advances in communication and technology have facilitated the practicalities of working across borders. Critical communication, however, should also help uncover the stories and histories of others. For example, in German society, the issue of antisemitism of refugees from Arab lands challenges the current approaches to antisemitism targeted at Germans. Antisemitism expressed by Arab migrants from Israeli-occupied Palestine is linked to global politics and divisions over the current Israel-Palestinian conflict. This conflict can be traced back to the various agreements created by the then British and French colonial powers. Critically addressing this antisemitism requires acknowledging people's histories but also enabling them to critically analyse their past and to develop strategies to resist oppression in a meaningful manner. Antisemitism is racism that denies the humanities of those who are racist as well as those who are victims of racism. Social workers can play a significant role in understanding these forms of antisemitism and developing relevant strategies to counteract them.

Social work practice and roles should not be limited by systems of welfare and legislation that exclude people. Rather, social workers should work toward changing and advocating the development of legislation and welfare systems to include the rights of vulnerable groups. For example, termination of pregnancies for non-medical reasons was illegal in the Republic of Ireland resulting in many women having to seek expensive options elsewhere or risk their lives by using unregulated procedures. The change in the legislation for legal abortions in 2018 was the result of years of campaigning by many Irish women. Before the new legislation, social workers faced considerable ethical and professional dilemmas in working with women who wanted access to abortion. Legislation often fails to reflect the changing contexts and realities of people's lives, as evident in this abortion example, where Irish women fought for this change for years. Social workers should work toward enabling vulnerable people to bring about social change.

The profession's commitment to human rights and its institutions, provides existing opportunities for solidarity and a common political platform. Student, academic, and practitioner exchange programs, and social media and digital exchange, have increased opportunities for sharing new ways of doing and thinking and forging professional solidarity. Social workers could play a central role in developing policy at global and local levels as they have the knowledge of structures and systems; as well as an understanding of the contemporary realities of people's lives.

In the changing context of practice, many social workers, trained in particular national contexts, are increasingly working in other nations; for example, British social workers employed in Canada, Australian social workers in the UK, Indian social workers in Australia. Social workers now increasingly work in statutory organisations, as well as in NGOs, in other countries such as the UN agencies, the Red Cross, Oxfam and Save the Children. Such exchange is beneficial as it brings diversity of ideas, energies, knowledge, skills and understanding. However, these movements also bring challenges and tensions. Social workers may have difficulties with working with certain groups or issues and may try to impose practices and ideas that are not suited to the local context or particular cultural group. For example, these can include working with families on traditional or cultural issues relating to child discipline, or marriage choices for younger people.

Working with different groups either in one's own country or in another country requires some level of understanding of that culture and their history. This skill is referred to as 'cultural or inter-cultural' competency within social work. Culturally competent work must seek to support indigenous ways of perceiving the world through an examination of power (critical), privilege (reflexivity), self-awareness (reflection) and a commitment to change (transformative practice) (Anand and Das, 2014).

Appreciating and respecting diversity (not only race and ethnicity but also poverty, disability, gender, age and sexuality), while addressing structural oppression remains a central concern for social work practice.

Global mindedness and professional practice

The scope of global minded practice includes global minded research and education. Professional practice is the culmination of complex processes including research and evaluation, theory application, education and social reform. Making distinctions between social work roles such as practitioner, administrator, educator and researcher is increasingly unrealistic given the demands of health and social care work. Practicing social workers are required to not only undertake interventions, but also create, explain, educate on and evaluate the interventions delivered. For example in Australia, hospital social work plays a vital role in the discharge planning of frail elderly patients from hospital. Social workers are required by health and social care management to demonstrate how intervention decreases the number of expensive and traumatic readmissions to hospital for these patients. Together with other members of the health professional's team, such as occupational therapists, physiotherapists, medics and nurses, hospital social workers are expected to clearly articulate their roles and contributions within multidisciplinary teams. The multiple roles undertaken by social workers are outlined in the diagram below (Figure 7.1).

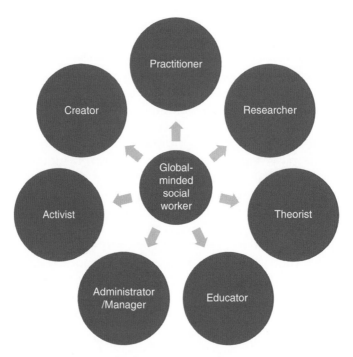

Figure 7.1: Multiple Roles within Social Work Practice

It is not only that social workers' roles and the contexts of their work differ, but the understanding of who is eligible to be given the title of 'social worker' also varies significantly across countries. In most countries of the global north, the identity of a social worker is framed by particular criteria, such as completion of an acknowledged education program or degree, undertaking so many hours of praxis and training or registration to a professional association. However, in many other countries, allied workers use the title 'social workers'. This includes a range of people such as community workers, voluntary workers, aid workers, philanthropic workers and so on. Most professionals would advocate that only those who have completed specific training should be recognised as a social worker; however, there has always been an argument that the profession should be inclusive of colleagues with similar goals, knowledge base and experience, irrespective of training. Creating fruitful and positive partnerships, respecting and learning from different but allied disciplines, may serve to enhance the profession's diversity. Being a global minded social worker should be about inclusion and pushing the boundaries to include multiple forms of knowledge, actors and roles.

Critical practice is extremely challenging and sometimes overwhelming. It is, therefore, extremely important that social workers practice routine self-care and seek support and supervision when appropriate. A key source of support, often overlooked is the support of peers. Self-reflection is an essential element in all social work practice. Opportunities to reflect in teams with other peers, particularly across borders, are underutilised. Exchange across borders can facilitate learning about different strategies and ways of working, and provides a unique opportunity to reflect. Unfortunately, very few programmes enable practitioners to participate in exchange as a tool to connect with other peers. Exchange opportunities may be sourced locally, but improved technology and global professional associations offer immense opportunities for social workers to travel to and collaborate with international colleagues. Nevertheless, the availability of social work exchange programs have been promoted by university schools of social work as valuable learning opportunities. Students are able to explore similarities and differences between local and global issues and practices together with the positionality of social work in other countries (Anand and Das, 2014).

However, a limitation of many exchange programs is the lack of equality between participating institutions. It is often the case that only researchers, educators, students and practitioners from 'developed' countries visit their peers in 'developing' countries. A bias is inherent in such an exchange giving the partner with the resources the freedom and ability to set the agenda, and they benefit the most from the opportunity. Such imbalances are problematic as they do not offer practitioners from developing countries similar opportunities to learn and critique. Understanding other perspectives and practices of social work across borders is challenging, particularly due to the use of language and concepts, the priorities set and the dominance of mainstream discourses. Reflection on issues of power in such exchanges programs and collaborative relationships should be a requirement of any mutual and reciprocal exchange program. Attention should be given to intentions of the participants involved, the expressed outcomes or goals, a reflection of the voices that are included and excluded as well as an acknowledgement of other discourses, for all involved parties of the exchange. The values and principles of global mindedness outlined are suitable for application to exchange and mobility programs as guidance for both students and academic staff.

Global mindedness in research

Global minded practice is informed by evidence and research findings. It is essential that the profession is able to demonstrate the impact of intervention and the processes toward the empowerment of people. It is of utmost importance that we as professionals do no harm to individuals, communities and society. Yet the extent to which evidence should be the sole determinant of practice, and what type of evidence is prioritised is contentious. Internationalisation and globalisation have tended to promote positivism and more scientific or quantitative approaches to research as opposed to qualitative methods. The current argument that social work should aim to be more scientific, evidence-based or evidence-informed eclipses past debates as to whether social work is a science, an applied science or an art. In many Scandinavian and European countries social work is taught in universities of applied sciences or technology, but involving creative, humanitarian and relationship practices, that reflect the practical nature of social work interventions. In other countries, such as the UK, Australia, Canada and the USA, social work is an established discipline aligned with other social sciences. In the UK, social work is considered an evidence-based activity. The notion of social work as an art form and the privileging of indigenous knowledge appear to sit in juxtaposition to dominant scientific aspirations. Yet as we have argued in this book, it is the acceptance of diverse ways of thinking and doing that can enhance the professions' relevance and resilience in the face of globalisation.

Qualitative and quantitative research traditions may best be understood as two sides of one coin, contributing to different understandings as to the causality of social injustice and impact of inequality. Social worker students and practitioners therefore require proficiency in both traditions, and need to remain critical of the limitations and strengths of both. Promoting the use of mixed methods, combining both methods of data collection, offers one solution to the binary approach to social sciences and health research. The existing skills of social workers in quantitative research methodology should not be undervalued in light of the dominance of quantitative or big data studies. Social workers, by nature of their clinical training, possess well-developed skills in interviewing, focus works, the analysis of narratives and in studying difficult-to-reach groups of people, which makes them excellent researchers. Social workers also have first-hand practical experience and knowledge of delivering complex social interventions and undertaking the evaluation of outcomes (i.e. formative, summative and contextual evaluation). Action research, participatory research and service evaluation are research methods that serve to promote global mindedness through the dissemination and sharing of practice results.

Research is an increasingly global enterprise, predominantly promoted by funding from the global north. Collaboration presents both new international opportunities as well as concerning implications for the exploitation of local subjects and issues. Both universities and funding organisations promote international collaborations as well as projects that have international impact. Global collaboration and comparative studies in social work offer an opportunity to address the professions diversity and a means of understanding how context shapes social problems and practice responses. International collaboration in social work research helps to builds local capacity, offers critical insights and creates new opportunities for exchange. Yet the pitfalls of international collaboration involve the prompting of dominant research approaches (representing another form of colonisation) that tend to overlook cultural differences (language, meaning, contexts). The disregard of different research traditions and ignorance of ethical and moral responsibility frequently results in a general lack of integrity, trust and respect (Anderson, 2010; Tuhiwai Smith, 1999) between international partners. Global mindedness in collaborative processes requires considerable planning, attention to methodology (Padget, 2016), an understanding of inter-cultural communication, power and politics, different resources and priorities, and considerable opportunities for critical reflection (Jandt, 2004). Academic publishing practices have presented new challenges for global minded academics. The most prestigious social work articles often lack a truly international profile of authors and topics.

Global mindedness in theory building

The current preoccupation with scientific findings has detracted attention from the need to convert statistics and results into theories of practice or guidelines for international practice. It is clear that social work draws from other social sciences such as sociology, psychology, education and social policy. However, we believe social workers have a role in bringing their practice experiences to research and the development of theory. Theory building and circular research processes that link practice to theory and practice to theory help to promote understanding and more discourse among social workers, internationally. As outlined in the earlier chapters, there are critical theories such as transnationalism, post-colonial and post-modern theories that seek to de-colonialise research methods and avoid imposing Eurocentric perspectives onto subjects. The building and development of theories and approaches will help frame the future of transformative social work.

Social work can, we believe, confidently contribute to building critical praxis-orientated theories in respect to communities, diversity, power, sustainability, policy, human rights and welfare issues. In fact, the emerging literature on ethics, human rights, oppression and power from social workers and social work academics, along with the global organisations of social workers, appears to be a step in this direction. Global minded practitioners should not limit their professional role to the collection of data but should take an active position in helping to analysis data and developing theory. While global mindedness is a part of the process to bring about change, social workers need to be able to change their practices to reflect the growing needs of people around the world and to engage in the global–local nexus in new ways.

Global mindedness in social work education

While international social work and exchange is gaining increasing attention, there is little that anchors its goals and purpose to a comprehensive program integral to social work education. International exchange programs and experiences are often provided in addition to the formal curriculum and in our experience only attract the more adventurous or global minded students and academic staff. We argue that this is a counter-productive stance as the concepts of international social work and global mindedness are central to future directions in social work practice. As argued in this book, global mindedness is embedded in anti-oppressive social work practice and linked to core social work values and skills. Unfortunately, social work education continues to narrowly focus on nationalistic priorities to determine curricula content and fails to do justice to local or global issues. Furthermore, social work programs which concentrate on local priorities to determine professional skills and knowledge are in danger of reducing professional education to training.

Dominelli (2007) has rightly noted that there is little emphasis on imparting an in-depth understanding of human rights in social work education. Addressing all categories of rights from the community level, as well as national or international level, is fundamental in global mindedness. Course content in social work education on the impact of internationalisation on the social work profession and international social work remains underdeveloped and limited. There is a need to educate professionals to be able to consider the roles and scope of social work beyond local interventions and settings. A failure to do so jeopardises the relevance and future of the profession and its goals of liberation, social justice. The world is changing at a hectic pace and social workers need to match their efforts for change in this changing world. It is conceivable that global mindedness may be accepted as a core competency in social education and practice and we would hope that our pragmatic approach to global mindedness would help facilitate that outcome.

Summary

Given the aggressive nature of globalisation, we can predict an increase in need for global minded social workers able to negotiate local, national and international contexts. The nature and trajectory of social phenomena, such as forced immigration, austerity, climate change, environmental issues and populism will result in more opportunities for increased trans-national and interconnected practice. Inequality among citizens of nation states and between countries of the north and south is growing exponentially and social workers have greater opportunities for structural work promoting social justice.

Yet, throughout this book we have posed critical questions as to the relevancy of social work in an increasingly globalised world. Our response has been to encourage social workers to push the geographical, administrative and ideological boundaries and to work on various issues, across various levels, with various partners, using methods that are informed, well theorised and well researched. We have encouraged social practitioners to push the traditional fields of practice and to think in terms of protection, diversity, structural reform and diversity. We envisage a profession that is true to its goals of supporting people in improving their quality of life and addressing inequality and oppression both globally and in local contexts. Existing professional organisations and networks provide a political platform for global social work in response to social, cultural and economic challenges. The profession has the benefits of diverse traditions, resources and skills from which to draw upon for the criticality, flexibility, creativity required for a practice that is more futuristic.

This book is one such attempt at problem-based learning using case examples to enable discussion and discourse on the bridging theory of global mindedness. More attempts at global mindedness are necessary and it remains imperative to develop clearer ideas, definitions and resources so as to further theorise international social work and apply this knowledge to practice. It is clear that this is an ongoing process.

In conclusion, it should be remembered that social work is the endeavour for a quality of life for all humanity. The project of social work is therefore global and the extent of interconnections and interdependencies have become more intricate and obvious, and present both challenges and opportunities for social work on a scale that the profession has not necessarily encountered before.

The commonality of purpose among social workers all around the world allows social workers to work together in creative and inspirational ways to challenge oppression and inequality. The profession remains highly diverse with the capacity to work with a range of individuals, groups and communities, using theories from various disciplines and engaging with contested spaces in practice. It is within these spaces that there remains scope for further developments of theory, and scope to invigorate social work. Furthermore, the nature of social work is not simply about applying theories into practice but engaging with people in dynamic ways to propose relevant solutions.

References

Abebe, T. and S. Bessell (2011). Dominant Discourses, Debates and Silences on Child Labour in Africa and Asia, *Third World Quarterly*, 32(4): 765–86.

Abram, F.Y. and A. Cruce (2007). A Reconceptualization of 'Reverse Mission' for International Social Work Education and Practice, *Social Work Education*, 26(1): 3–19.

ADCS (2018). Care Crisis Review Report. Published on 13.06.2018. Available at http://adcs.org.uk/care/article/care-crisis-review-report, accessed on 23.08.2018.

Akimoto, T. (2008). *What Is International Social Work? Its contribution to social work in a global society*. Symposium an der 100 Jahre Alice Salomon Hochschule Berlin am 24.10.2008. Available at https://www.ash-berlin.eu/100-Jahre-ASH/symposium/doc/3_5_akimoto.pdf , accessed on 24.4.2018.

All India Disaster Mitigation Institute (AIDMI) (2005). Tsunami, Gender and Recovery Special Issue for International Day for Disaster Risk Reduction. Available at http://www.Southasiadisasters.net/index%20tsu.htm, accessed on 13.12.2017.

Anand, J. and C. Das (2014). Strategies for Critical Reflection in International Contexts for Social Work Students, *International Social Work*, 57(2): 109–20.

Anand, J.C., Davidson, G., and Kelly, B. (2018). Personalization of care: a wicked problem or a wicked solution?. In W. Thomas. A. Hujala and S. Laulainen, R. McMurray, *The Management of Wicked Problems in Health and Social Care*. New York: Routledge: 60–74.

Anastas, J. (2007). Theorizing (In)Equity for Women in Social Work, *Affilia: Journal of Women and Social Work*, 22(3): 235–39. Available at http://journals.sagepub.com/doi/pdf/10.1177/0886109907302282, accessed on 23.08.2018.

Anderson, M. (2010). *International Research Collaborations: anticipating challenges instead of being surprised*, The Europa World of Learning. (ISBN 978-1-85743-567-2). Available at http://www.educationarena.com/pdf/sample/sample-essay-anderson.pdf, accessed on 7.12.2017.

Andreotti, V. (2006). Soft Versus Critical Global Citizenship Education, Global Citizenship, Policy and Practice, *Development Education Review*, 3: 40–51. Available at https://www.developmenteducationreview.com/issue/issue-3/soft-versus-critical-global-citizenship-education, accessed on 29.8.2017.

Andreotti, V. O., Biesta, G. and Ahenakew, C. (2015). Between the Nation and the Globe education for global mindedness in Finland, *Journal of Globalisation,*

Societies and Education, 13 (2:Work, Learning and Transnational Migration): 246–259.

Annan, K. (1997). The Universal Declaration of Human Rights Enshrines and Illuminates Global Pluralism and Diversity, Says Secretary-General on the 50th Anniversary of the Declaration, United Nations Secretary-General, Speech in Teheran delivered by Kofe Annan on 12.10.1997. Available at https://www.un.org/sg/en/content/sg/speeches/1997-12-10/universal-declaration-human-rights-enshrines-and-illuminates-global, accessed on 23.08.2018.

Antonucci, T.C., J.S. Jackson and S. Biggs (2007). Intergenerational Relations: Theory, Research, and Policy, *Journal of Social Issues*, 63(4): 679–93.

APASWE/IASSW (2011). *International Definition of Social Work Review*, APASWE/IASSW Asian and Pacific Regional Workshop (4.11.2010). Social Work Research Institute Asian Center for Welfare in Society. Japan College of Social Work.

Ashley, H., N. Kenton and H. Milligan (eds) (2012). *Participatory Learning and Action Biodiversity and Culture: Exploring Community Protocols, Rights and Consent.* London: The International Institute for Environment and Development (IIED).

Asia Pacific Forum on Women, Labour and Development (APWLD) (2005a). *Tsunami Aftershocks: Gender Perspective Needed in Disaster Management*, Forum 18 (1). Available online at: http://www.apwld.org/vol181—01.htm, accessed 17.05.2006.

Asia Pacific Forum on Women, Labour and Development (APWLD) (2005b). *Why are Women More Vulnerable during Disasters. Women's Human Rights in the Tsunami Aftermath.* Bangkok: APWLD.

Banks, S. (2012). *Ethics and Values in Social Work.* Basingstoke: Palgrave Macmillan.

Barn, R. and C. Das (2015). Family Group Conferences and Cultural Competence in Social Work, *British Journal of Social Work*. Published online. Available at http://bjsw.oxfordjournals.org/cgi/reprint/bcu105?ijkey=zWz7tNI5MtzdACX&keytype=ref, accessed on 18.12.2018.

BBC (2017). Grenfell fire: Rebuilding trust in council to 'take a generation'. Report, 12 July. Available at http://www.bbc.com/news/uk-40580176, accessed on 12.12.2017.

BBC (2018). Heterosexual couple win civil partnership case, 27.06.2018. Available at https://www.bbc.com/news/uk-44627990, accessed on 23.08.2018.

Ben-Ari, A. and R. Strier (2010). Rethinking Cultural Competence: What Can We Learn from Levinas, *British Journal of Social Work*, 40(7): 2155–67.

Betancourt, J.R., A.R. Green, J.E. Carrillo and E.R. Park (2005). Cultural Competence and Health Care Disparities: Key Perspectives and Trends, *Health Affairs*, 24(2): 499–505.

Bhabha, H. (2012) *The Location of Culture*. Routledge. ISBN 0-415-33639-2.

Biggart, A. (2008). National Youth Policy in the UK: Trends, Issues and Evaluation. In A. Ittel, L. Stecher, H. Merkens and J. Zinnecker (eds), *Jahrbuch Jugendforschung*, Ausgabe 7. 2007. Wiesbaden: Verlag für Sozialwissenschaften GWV Fachverlage GmbH: 385–406.

Bilge, S. (2010). Beyond Subordination vs. Resistance: An Intersectional Approach to the Agency of Veiled Muslim Women, *Journal of Intercultural Studies*, 31(1): 9–28.

Billig, M. (1995). *Banal Nationalism*. London: Sage Publications.

Bogo, M. and W. Herington (1988). Consultation in Social Work Education in the International Context, *International Social Work*, 31(4): 305–16.

Borowski, A. (2007). *Longevity and Social Change in Australia*. Sydney: University of NSW Press.

Bowes, A. and B. Daniel (2010). Introduction: Interrogation Harm and Abuse: A Life Span Approach, *Social Policy and Society*, 9(2): 221–9.

Brand, D., T. Reith and D. Statham (2005). *Core Roles and Tasks of Social Workers. A Scoping Study for the GSCC*. London: General Social Care Council.

Brennan, T. (2006). The economic image-function of the periphery. In A. Loomba, K. Survir, M. Bunzl (eds), *Postcolonialism and Beyond*. Delhi: Permanent Black: 101–122.

Brennan, E. (2010). *Definitions for Social Sustainability and Social Work Paper*. White paper distributed for CSWE conference, Portland State University.

Burger, P. and T. Luckman (1966). *The Social Construction of Reality: A Treatise in the Sociology of Knowledge*. Garden City, NY: Penguin Books.

Burns, K. (2005) *Gender Dimensions of the Response to the Tsunami*, paper presented on behalf of the United Nations Office for the Coordination of Humanitarian Affairs (OCHA), Tsunami Health Conference, Phuket, Thailand (4–6 May).

Butler, I. and C. Hickman (2011). *Social Work with Children and Families: Getting into Practice*. 3rd edn. London: Jessica Kingsley Publishers.

Campbell, J., Duffy, J., Traynor, C., Coulter, S., Reilly, I and Pinkerton, J. (2013). Social Work Education and Political Conflict: Preparing Students to Address the Needs of Victims and Survivors of the Troubles in Northern Ireland, *European Journal of Social Work*, 16 (4): 506–520.

Carniol, B. (1992). Structural Social Work: Maurice Moreau's Challenge to Social Work Practice, *Journal of Progressive Human Services*, 3(1): 1–20.

Carter Anand, J., G. Davidson, G. Macdonald and B. Kelly (2012). The Transition to Personal Budgets for People with Disabilities: A Review of Practice in Specified Jurisdictions. A National Disability Authority Working Paper. London: National Disability Authority. Available at http://www.inis.gov.ie/website/nda/cntmgmtnew.Nsf/0/F6E10844509D45B780257B3C00517FB4/$File/personal_budgets_state_of_evidence_nov_2012.htm, accessed on 23.8.2018.

Carter, C. (2014). 28 July 1586: Britain is introduced to the potato. *Money Week* (28.7.2014). Available at https://moneyweek.com/28-july-1586-britain-is-introduced-to-the-potato/, accessed on 13.12.2017.

Castells, M. (1999). *Information Technology, Globalization and Social Development*, UNRISD Discussion Paper No. 114. Geneva: United Nations Research Institute for Social Development (UNRISD).

Castells, M. (2010). The Rise of the Fourth World: Informational Capitalism, Poverty, and Social Exclusion, *End of Millennium: With a New Preface*, Volume III, 2nd edn. Oxford, UK: Wiley-Blackwell, Chapter 2.

Castle, S. (2002). International Migration at the Beginning of the Twenty-First Century: Global Trends and Issues, *International Social Science Journal*, 52(165): 269–81.

Castles, S. (2004). The Factors that Make and Unmake Migration Policies, *International Migration Review*, 38(3): 852–84.

Chau, R.C.M., S.W.K. Yu and C.T.L. Tran (2011). The Diversity Based Approach to Culturally Sensitive Practices, *International Social Work*, 54(1): 21–33.

Cheyne, C., M. O'Brien and M. Belgrave (2005). *Social Policy in Aotearoa New Zealand: A Critical Introduction*, 3rd edn. Melbourne: Oxford University Press.

Christie, A. (2006). Negotiating the Uncomfortable Intersections between Gender and Professional Identities to Social Work, *Critical Social Policy*, 26(2): 390–411.

Clarke, J. and J. Newman (1997). *The Managerial State*. London: Sage Publications.

Coates, J. (2003). *Ecology and Social Work: Toward a New Paradigm*. Halifax, NS: Fernwood.

Colas, A. (1997). The Promises of International Civil Society, *Global Society*, 11(3): 261–77.

Colleen, L. (2004). *Social Work and Social Justice: A Structural Approach to Practice*. Canada: University of Toronto Press.

The Conversation (2014). Muslim Feminists Reclaim the Hijab to Fight the Patriarchy, *The Conversation*, 5.9.2014. Available at https://theconversation.com/muslim-feminists-reclaim-the-hijab-to-fight-the-patriarchy-31126?sa=pg2&sq=hijab&sr=3, accessed 4.7.2017.

The Conversation (2015). German Court Rules Against Banning Veil in Schools but Europe Remains Divided, *The Conversation*, 23.3.2015) Available at https://theconversation.com/german-court-rules-against-banning-veil-in-schools-but-europe-remains-divided-39077?sa=pg2&sq=hijab&sr=6, accessed 4.7.2017.

The Conversation (2016). Hard Evidence: Muslim women and discrimination in Britain, *The Conversation*, 1.4.2016. Available at https://theconversation.com/hard-evidence-muslim-women-and-discrimination-in-britain-56446?sa=pg2&sq=hijab&sr=7 , accessed 4.7.2017.

Cook, R. (2001). Robin Cook's chicken tikka masala speech. *The Guardian*, 19.4.2001. Available at https://www.theguardian.com/world/2001/apr/19/race.britishidentity, accessed on 13.12.2017.

Cook, S. and E. Dugarova (2014). Rethinking Social Development for a Post-2015 *World Development*, 57 (1). Available at http://www.un.org/esa/socdev/egms/docs/2014/SessionVCookDugarovaRethinkingsocialdevelopment.pdf , accessed on 5.7.2018.

Cooper, C., A. Selwood, and G. Livingston (2009). Knowledge, detection, and reporting of abuse by health and social care professionals: A systematic review, *American Journal of Geriatric Psychiatry*, 17: 826–838.

Cuinhane, C.E. (2006). *Papel da instrução escolar na inserção socioprofissional dos jovens no ercado de trabalho em Moçambique: O caso da cidade de Maputo* [The role of school instruction on the south socio-professional insertion in the employment market – The case of Maputo city]. Licentiate dissertation presented at Eduardo Mondlane University (UEM); Maputo- Mozambique (Unpublished document).

Dahlkild-Öhman, G. and M. Eriksson (2013). Inequality Regimes and Men's Positions in Social Work, *Gender, Work and Organization*, 20(1): 85–100. Available at https://onlinelibrary.wiley.com/doi/pdf/10.1111/j.1468-0432.2011.00572.x, accessed on 23.08.2018.

Dale, S. and R. Brown, (2006). How Does Cash and Counselling Affect Costs?, *Health Services Research*, 42(1): 488–509.

Daly, J. and A. Coffey (2010). Staff Perceptions of Elder Abuse, *Nursing Older People*, 22(4): 33–37.

Das, C. and J. Anand (2016). Pushing Theory: Applying Cultural Competence in Practice – A Case Study of Community Conflict in NI. In C. Williams and M. Graham (eds), *Social Work in a Diverse Society*, University of Bristol: Policy Press, Chapter 2.

Das, C., M. O'Niell and J. Pinkerton (2015). Re-Engaging with Community Work as A Method of Practice in Social Work: A View from Northern Ireland (NI), *Journal of Social Work*, 16(2): 196–215.

Davis, G. (2004). *A History of the Social Development Network in the World Bank*. Washington, DC: The World Bank Social Development, Paper No.56.

Department of Health (2009). *No Secrets: Guidance on Developing and Implementing Multi-Agency Policies and Procedures to Protect Vulnerable Adults from Abuse*. London: Department of Health.

Derrida, J. (1976). *Of Grammatology*. Baltimore: John Hopkins University Press.

Deutsche Welle (2018). German food banks under pressure. *Deutsche Welle*, 19.03.2018. Available at https://www.dw.com/en/german-food-banks-under-pressure/av-43019467, accessed on 23.08.2018.

Devaney, C. and Mc Gregor, C. (2017). Child protection and family support practice in Ireland: a contribution to present debates from a historical perspective. *Child & Family Social Work*, 22: 1255–1263.

Dobson, A. (2005). Globalisation, cosmopolitanism and the Environment, *International Relations*,19: 259–273.

Dominelli, L. (2004a). International Social Work Education at the Crossroads, *Social Work and Society: International Online Journal*, 2(1). Available at http://www.socwork.net/sws/article/view/233.

Dominelli, L. (2004b). *Social Work: Theory and Practice for a Changing Profession*. Malden, MA: Polity Press.

Dominelli, L. (2005). International Social Work: Themes and Issues for the 21st Century, *International Social Work*, 48(4): 504–07.

Dominelli, L. (2007). Human Rights in Social Work Practice: An Invisible Part of the Social Work Curriculum? In E. Reichert (ed.), *Challenges in Human Rights: A Social Work Perspective*, New York: Columbia University Press, pp 16–43.

Dominelli, L. (2010). Globalization, Contemporary Challenges and Social Work Practice, *International Social Work*, 53(5): 599–612.

Dominelli, L. (2012). *Green Social Work: From Environmental Crises to Environmental Justice*. Cambridge: Polity Press.

Dominelli, L. (2014a). Internationalizing Professional Practices: The Place of Social Work in the International Arena, *International Social Work*, 57(3): 258–67.

Dominelli, L. (2014b). Promoting Environmental Justice through Green Social Work Practice: A Key Challenge for Practitioners and Educators, *International Social Work*, 57(4): 338–45.

Dominelli, L. (2015). The Opportunities and Challenges of Social Work Interventions in Disaster Situations, *International Social Work*, 58(5): 659–72.

Dominelli, L. and J. Campling (2002). *Anti-Oppressive Social Work: Theory and Practice*. Hampshire Basingstoke and New York: Palgrave Macmillan.

Dominelli, L. and M. Moosa-Mitha (eds) (2014). *Reconfiguring Citizenship, Social Exclusion and Diversity within Inclusive Citizenship Practices*. Contemporary Social Work Studies. Aldershot: Ashgate.

Donnelly, J. (2007). The Relative Universality of Human Rights, *Human Rights Quarterly*, 29(2): 281–306.

Donnelly, M. (1999). Assessing the Quality of Care for the Elderly using the SERVQUAL Approach and Modified Instruments, Proceedings of the First Scottish Trade Union Research Network Conference: 104–9. Paisley: STUC.

Douglas, H. (2005). The Development of Practice Theory in Adult Protection Intervention: Insights from a Recent Research Project, *The Journal of Adult Protection*, 7(1): 32–45.

Douzinas, C. (2007). *Human Rights and Empire: The Political Philosophy of Cosmopolitanism*. Abingdon, Oxford and New York: Routledge-Cavendish.

Dow, B. and M. Joosten (2012). Understanding Elder Abuse: A Social Rights Perspective, *International Psychogeriatrics*, 24(6): 853–55.

Downey, L., E. Bonds and K. Clark (2010). Natural Resource Extraction, Armed Violence, and Environmental Degradation, *Organization & Environment*, 23(4): 417–45.

Drolet, J., L. Dominelli, M. Alston, R. Ersing, G. Mathbor and H. Wu (2015). Women Rebuilding Lives Post-Disaster: Innovative Community Practices for Building Resilience and Promoting Sustainable Development, *Gender & Development*, 23(3): 433–48.

Dustin, D. (2007). *The McDonaldization of Social Work*. Aldershot: Ashgate.

Egan, D. (2008). Issues Concerning Direct Payments in the Republic of Ireland. A report for the Person Centre. Available at http://www.enil.eu/wp-content/uploads/2012/11/Draft-Ireland-Report-on-Direct-Payments-text-version.doc, accessed on 3.1.2019.

Elhage, A. (2016). Keeping Children in the Family Instead of Foster Care, Institute for Family Studies. Published on 18.08.2016. Available at https://ifstudies.org/blog/keeping-children-in-the-family-instead-of-foster-care, accessed on 23.08.2018.

El Guindi, F. (1999). *Veil: Modesty, Privacy and Resistance*. Oxford: Berg Publishers.

Emerson, E., and Hatton, C. (1998). Residential provision for people with intellectual disabilities in England, Wales and Scotland. *Journal of Applied Research in Intellectual Disabilities*, 11: 1–14.

Esping-Andersen, G. (1999). *Social Foundations of Postindustrial Economies*. Oxford: OUP.

Esping-Andersen, G. (2013). *The Three Worlds of Welfare Capitalism*. Cambridge: Polity Press.

Evans, C. (1995). Disability, Discrimination and Local Authority Social Service 2: User's Perspectives. In G. Zarb (ed.), *Removing Disabling Barriers*, London: Policy Studies Institute: 116–23.

Evans, T. (2010). *Professional Discretion in Welfare Services beyond Street-Level Bureaucracy*. London: Routledge.

FAO (2011). *Global Food Losses and Food Waste: Extent Causes and Prevention*. Rome: Food and Agriculture Organization of the United Nations.

FAO (2015). *The State of Food Insecurity in the World: Meeting the 2015 International Hunger Targets: Taking Stock of Uneven Progress*. Rome: Food and Agriculture Organization of the United Nations.

Faux, J. (2006). *The Global Class War: How America's Bipartisan Elite Lost Our Future and What It Will Take to Win It Back*. Hoboken, NJ: John Wiley & Sons, Inc.

Fisher, K., R. Gleeson, R. Edwards, C. Purcal, T. Sitek, B. Dinning, et al. (2010). *Effectiveness of individual funding approaches for disability support*. Canberra: Department of Families, Housing, Community Services and Indigenous Affairs, Commonwealth of Australia.

Fletcher, L.E., E. Stover and H.M. Weinstein(eds (2005). *After the Tsunami. Human Rights of Vulnerable Populations*. Berkeley, CA: East-West Centre, University of California.

Foucault, M. (1980). *Power/Knowledge: Selected Interviews and Other Writings 1972–1977*. New York: Pantheon Books.

Freeman, M.A. (2004). *Environmental Security in the Global Capitalist System: A World-Systems Approach and Study of Panama*, BA thesis. Orlando, FL: University of Central Florida.

Furlong, M. and J. Wight (2011). Promoting 'Critical Awareness' and 'Critiquing Cultural': Towards Disrupting Received Professional Knowledges, *Australian Social Work*, 64(1): 38–54.

Gaine, C. (2010). *Equality and Diversity in Social Work Practice* (Transforming Social Work Practice Series). Exeter: Learning Matters Ltd.

Galpin, D. and N. Bates (2009). *Social Work Practice with Adults* (Transforming Social Work Practice Series). Exeter: Learning Matters Ltd.

George, P. and S. Marlowe (2005). Structural Social Work in Action: Experiences from Rural India, *Journal of Progessive Human Services*, 16(1): 5–24.

Giarrusso, R., M. Silverstein and V.L. Bengtson (1996). Family Complexity and the Grandparent Role, *Generations*, 20(1): 17–23.

Giddens, A. (2009). *The Politics of Climate Change*. Cambridge, UK: Polity.

Gigauri, G. (2013). Potential Contradictions Between Democratic and Human Rights Processes in the Area of Migration and Asylum, *European Scientific Journal*, special edition. Available at http://eujournal.org/index.php/esj/article/view/1612/1615.

Gray, M. (2005). Dilemmas of International Social Work: Paradoxical Processes in Indigenisation, Universalism and Imperialism, *International Journal of Social Welfare*, 14(3): 231–38.

Gray, M. and J. Coates (2010). 'Indigenization' and Knowledge Development: Extending the Debate, *International Social Work*, 53(5): 613–27.

Gray, M. and J. Fook (2004). The Quest for a Universal Social Work: Some Issues and Implications, *Social Work Education*, 23(5): 625–44.

Gray, M. and S. Webb (2008). Debate: Social Work as Art Revisited, *International Journal of Social Welfare*, 17: 182–93.

Gray, M. and S. Webb (2012). *Social Work Theories and Methods*. London: Sage.

Gray, M., J. Midgley and B. Webb (2012). *The Sage Handbook of International Social Work*. London: Sage Publications.

Green, S. and E. Baldry (2008). Building Indigenous Australian Social Work, *Australian Social Work*, 61(4): 389–402.

Guy, J. (2009). What is Global and What is Local? A Theoretical Discussion around Globalization, *Parsons, Journal of Information Mapping*, 1(2): 1–16.

Gyimah-Brempong, K. and M.S. Kimenyi (2013). *Oyuth Policy and the Future of African Development. Africa Growth Initiative at Brookings*. Washington, DC: Brookings.

Hall, E.T. (1959). *The Silent Language*. New York: Doubleday.

Harbison, J. and M. Morrow (1998). Re-Examining the Social Construction of 'Elder Abuse and Neglect': A Canadian Perspective, *Ageing and Society*, 18(6): 691–711.

Hare, I. (2004). Defining Social Work for the 21st Century: The International Federation of Social Workers' Revised Definition of Social Work, *International Social Work*, 47(3): 407–24.

Hareven, T.K. (ed), (2012) Aging and Generational Relations over the Life Course. Berlin: de Gruyter, Polity Press: 462–82.

Harf, A., S. Skandrani, J. Sibeoni, C. Pontvert, A. Revah-Levy and M.R. Moro (2015). Cultural Identity and Internationally Adopted Children: Qualitative Approach to Parental Representations, *PLoS ONE*, 10(3): e0119635.

Harlow, E. (2004). Why Don't Women Want to Be Social Workers Anymore? New Managerialism, Postfeminism and the Shortage of Social Workers in Social Services Departments in England and Wales, *European Journal of Social Work*, 7(2): 167–79.

Harrison, G. and R. Turner (2011). Being a 'Culturally Competent' Social Worker: Making Sense of a Murky Concept in Practice, *British Journal of Social Work*, 41(2): 333–50.

Hathaway, J.C. (2014). Food Deprivation: A Basis for Refugee Status? *Social Research*, 81(2): 327–39.

Hatton, C. and J. Waters (2011). *The National Personal Budget Survey, Think Local Act Personal*. London: In Control Publications.

Haug, E. (2005). Critical Reflections on the Emerging Discourse of International Social Work, *International Social Work*, 48(2): 126–35.

Healy, K. (2014). *Social Work Theories in Context: Creating Frameworks for Practice*. Basingstoke: Palgrave Macmillan.

Healy, L. (2001). *International Social Work: Professional Action in an Interdependent World*. Oxford: Oxford University Press.

Healy, L.M. and R.J. Linkeds (2011). *Handbook of International Social Work: Human Rights, Development and the Global Profession*. Oxford: Oxford University Press.

Hennig, B. (2017). Country File: Mapping rural-to-urban migration. Available at http://geographical.co.uk/places/mapping/item/2084-country-file, accessed on 23.08.2018.

Hicks, A. and L. Kenworthy (2003). Varieties of Welfare Capitalism, *Socio-Economic Review*, 1(1): 26–61.

Hightower, J., M.J. Smith and H.C. Hightower (2006). Hearing the Voice of Abused Older Women, *Journal of Gerontological Social Work*, 46(3/4): 205–27.

Hoff, M.D. and R.J. Polack (1993). Social Dimensions of the Environmental Crisis: Challenges for Social Work, *Social Work*, 38(2): 204–11.

Hoogvelt, A.M. (1997). *Globalisation and the Postcolonial World: The New Political Economy of Development*. Baltimore, MD: John Hopkins University Press.

Hugman, R. (2010). *Understanding International Social Work: A Critical Analysis*. Basingstoke: Palgrave Macmillan: 151.

Hussein S., Manthorpe J., and Penhale B. (2007). Public Perceptions of the Neglect and Mistreatment of Older People: findings of a United Kingdom survey. *Ageing and Society*, 27, 919–940.

IASSW–AIETS/IFSW/ICSW (2012). *The Global Agenda for Social Work and Social Development: Commitment to Action.* Available at http://cdn.ifsw.org/assets/globalagenda2012.pdf, accessed on 3.1.2019.

Ife, J. (2001). Local and Global Practice: Relocating Social Work as a Human Rights Profession in the New Global Order, *European Journal of Social Work*, 4(1): 5–15.

Ife, J. (2002). *Community Development: Community based Alternatives in an Age of Globalisation*, 2nd edn. Frenchs Forest, Australia: Longman.

Ife, J. (2007). Cultural Relativism and Community Activism. In E. Reichert (ed.), *Challenges in Human Rights: A Social Work Perspective.* New York: Columbia University Press: 76–96.

Ife, J. (2008). *Human Rights and Social Work: Towards Rights-Based Practice.* Cambridge: Cambridge University Press.

Ife, J. (2010). *Human Rights from Below: Achieving Rights through Community Development.* Melbourne: Cambridge University Press.

Ife, J. and L. Fiske (2006). Human Rights and Community Work: Complementary Theories and Practices, *International Social Work*, 49(3): 297–308.

IFSW/IASSW (2014). *Global Definition of Social Work.* IFSW and IASSW. Available at https://www.ifsw.org/global-definition-of-social-work/, accessed on 3.1.2019.

IFSW (2018). Global Social Work Statement of Ethical Practice. Available at https://www.ifsw.org/global-social-work-statement-of-ethical-principles/, accessed on 21.1.2019.

Jandt, F.E. (ed) (2004). *Intercultural Communication: A Global Reader.* Thousand Oaks, CA: Sage Publications.

Jordan, B. (1978). A Comment on 'Theory and Practice in Social Work', *British Journal of Social Work*, 8(11): 23–25.

Jordan, B. (2001). Tough Love: Social Work, Social Exclusion and the Third Way, *British Journal of Social Work*, 31: 527–46.

Karger, H., J. Owen and S. van de Graaf (2012). Governance and Disaster Management: The Governmental and Community Response to Hurricane Katrina and the Victorian Bushfires, *Social Development Issues*, 34(3): 30–49.

Kaseke, E. (1991). Social Work Practice in Zimbabwe, *Journal of Social Development in Africa*, 6(1): 33–45.

Kelly, G. and C. Das. (2012). Should Adoption Be an Option? In R. Sheehan and H. Rhoades (eds), *Vulnerable Children and the Law Children: International Evidence for improving Child Welfare, Child Protection and Children's Rights.* London/Philadelphia: Jessica Kinsley Publishers: 251–268.

Kempe, R.H. Sr. (2012). Engaging the Youth in Kenya: Empowerment, Education, and Employment, *International Journal of Adolescence and Youth*, 17(4): 221–36.

Kendall, K.A. (1979). Toward Reciprocity in Technical Assistance through Collegial Relationships, *International Social Work*, 22: 2–8.

Killick, C. and B.J. Taylor (2009). Professional Decision-Making on Elder Abuse: Systematic Narrative Review, *Journal of Elder Abuse and Neglect*, 21: 211–38.

Killick, C. and B.J. Taylor (2012). Judgements of Social Care Professionals on Elder Abuse Referrals: A Factorial Survey, *British Journal of Social Work*, 42(5): 814–32.

Kitwood, T. (1996). Building up the Mosaic of Good Practice, *Journal of Dement Care*, 3: 12–13.

Kohli, R. and F. Mitchell (eds) (2007). *Social Work with Unaccompanied Asylum-Seeking Children*, London: Palgrave Macmillan.

Kumagai, A.K. and M.L. Lypson (2009). Beyond Cultural Competence: Critical Consciousness, Social Justice, and Multicultural Education, *Academic Medicine*, 84(6): 782–87.

Lafferty, A., M.P. Treacy, G. Fealy, J. Drennan and I. Lyons (2012). *Older People's Experiences of Mistreatment and Abuse*. Dublin: NCPOP at University College Dublin.

Laird, S.E. (2012). The Construction of the Child in Ghanaian Welfare Policy in A. Twum-Danso and R. Ame (eds), *Childhoods at the Intersection of the Local and the Global*. Basingstoke: Palgrave Macmillan: 94–118.

Legal Services Commission of South Australia (2018). Who can adopt and be adopted? Last revised on 9.07.2018. Available at https://www.lawhandbook. sa.gov.au/ch21s11s05s01.php, accessed on 23.08.2018.

Levy, A. and J.G. Vaillancourt (2011). War on Earth? Junctures between Peace and the Environment. In T. Matyók, J. Senehi and S. Byrneeds (eds), *Critical Issues in Peace and Conflict Studies: Theory, Practice, and Pedagogy*. Lanham, MD: Lexington Books: 217–44.

Liebel, M. (2014). *Protecting the rights of working children instead of banning child labour: Bolivia tries a new legislation*, Internationale Akademie für innovative Pädagogik, Psychologie und Ökonomie GmbH, Freien Universität Berlin. Available at http://www.europarl.europa.eu/meetdocs/2014_2019/documents/ deve/dv/liebel_policy_paper_bolivia_/liebel_policy_paper_bolivia_en.pdf, accessed on 10.12.2017.

Livholts, M. and L. Bryant (2017). *Social Work in a Glocalised World*. Oxon and New York: Routledge.

Lorenz, W. (1994). *Social Work in a Changing Europe*. London: Routledge.

Lorenz, W. (2001). Soziale Arbeit: Internationale. In: H.-U. Otto and H. Thiersch, (eds), *Handbuch Sozialarbeit und Sozialpädagogik*, Neuwied/Kriftel (Luchterhand): 1644–1648.

Lorenz, W. (2004). *Towards a European Paradigm of Social Work – Studies in the History of Modes of Social Work and Social Policy in Europe*. (D.Phil.), Fakultät Erziehungswissenschaften, Technischen Universität Dresden. Available at http://webdoc.sub.gwdg.de/ebook/dissts/Dresden/Lorenz2005.pdf, accessed 29.8.2017.

Lundy, C. (2004). *Social Work and Social Justice: A Structural Approach to Practice*. Toronto: University of Toronto Press.

Lyons, K., K. Manion and M. Carlsen (2006). *International Perspectives on Social Work; Global Conditions and Local Practice*. Basingstoke: Palgrave Macmillan.

Lyons, K.H., T. Hokenstad, M. Pawar, N. Huegler and N. Hall (eds) (2012). *The Sage Handbook of International Social Work*. London: Sage.

Maidment, J. and S. Macfarlane (2008). Craft Groups: Sites of Friendship, Empowerment, Belonging and Learning for Older Women, *Groupwork*, 19(1): 10–25.

Maidment, J. and S. Macfarlane (2011). Crafting Communities: Promoting Inclusion, Empowerment, and Learning between Older Women, *Australian Social Work*, 64(3): 283–98.

Mapp, S., Boutte-Queen, N., Erich, S., and Taylor, P. (2008). Evidence-based practice or practice-based evidence: What is happening with MEPA and current adoption practices? *Families in Society*, 89(3): 375–384.

Martin, K. and B. Mirraboopa (2003). Ways of Knowing, Being and Doing: A Theoretical Framework and Methods for Indigenous and Indigenist Research, *Journal of Australian Studies*, 27(76): 203–14.

Mary, N. (2008). *Social Work in a Sustainable World*. Oxford: Oxford University Press.

McDonald, H., E. Graham-Harrison and S. Baker (2018) Ireland votes by land-slide to legalise abortion. *The Guardian*, 26.05.2018. Available at https://www.theguardian.com/world/2018/may/26/ireland-votes-by-landslide-to-legalise-abortion, accessed on 23.08.2018.

Midgley, J. (1981). *Professional Imperialism: Social Work in the Third World*. London: Heinemann.

Midgley, J. (1990). International Social Work: Learning from the Third World, *Social Work* 35(4): 295–301.

Midgley, J. (2001). Issues in International Social Work: Resolving Critical Debates in the Profession, *Journal of Social Work*, 1(1): 21–35.

Midgley, J., & Conley, A. (eds). (2010). *Social Work and Social Development: Theories and Skills for Developmental Social Workers*. New York, NY: Oxford University Press.

Moore, M. (1993). Indian village women fight state, husbands to ban liquor, *The Washington Post*, 13.12.1993. Available at https://www.washingtonpost.com/archive/politics/1993/12/19/indian-village-women-fight-state-husbands-to-ban-liquor/86848556-71c6-4e4d-a61a-2df9d604e341/?noredirect=on&utm_term=.025fd17f9823, accessed on 5.7.2018.

Moosa-Mitha, M. (2014). Using Citizenship Theory to Challenge Nationalist Assumptions in the Construction of International Social Work Education, *International Social Work*, 57(3): 201–08.

Moosa-Mitha, M. and F. Ross-Seriff (2010). Transnational Social Work and Lessons Learned from Transnational Feminism, *Affilia: Journal of Women and Social Work*, 25(2): 105–09.

Moreau, M.J. (1979). A Structural Approach to Social Work Practice. *Canadian Journal of Social Work Education*, 78–94.

Morelli, A.G., B. Rogoff, D. Oppenheim and D. Goldsmith (1992). Cultural Variation in Infants' Sleeping Arrangements: Questions of Independence, *Developmental Psychology*, 28(4): 604–13.

Mullaly, B. (2007). *The New Structural Social Work*, 3rd edn. Toronto, ON: Oxford University Press.

Munro, E. (2004). The Impact of Audit on Social Work Practice, *British Journal of Social Work*, 34(8): 1075–95.

Mupedziswa R. (1992). Africa at the Crossroads: Major Challenges for Social Work Education and Practice towards the Year 2000. *Journal of Social Development in Africa*, 7(2). doi 10.1177/0020872807088083.

Murray, K.M., and Hicks, S.F. (2013). Structural Social Work. In M. Gray & S.A. Webb (eds), *Social Work Theories and Methods*, 2nd edn. London: Sage: 110–125.

Nagy, G. and D. Falk (2000). Dilemmas in International and Cross-Cultural Social Work, *International Social Work*, 43(1): 49–60.

Netflix (2016). Episode 3: Exploit, from the series Dark Net.

O'Donnell, D., M.P. Treacy, G. Fealy, I. Lyons, A. Phelan, A. Lafferty, J. Drennan, S. Quin and A. O'Loughlin (2012). *Managing Elder Abuse in Ireland: The Senior Case Workers Experience*. Dublin: National Centre for the Protection of Older People.

OECD (2018). OECD iLibrary: Young Population (Indicator). doi: 10.1787/3d774f19-en, accessed on 14.12.2018.

ONS (2016). Overview of the UK Population: Feb 2016. Available at https://www.ons.gov.uk/peoplepopulationandcommunity/populationandmigration/populationestimates/articles/overviewoftheukpopulation/february2016#how-are-the-characteristics-of-the-uk-population-changing, accessed on: 14.12.2018.

Orme, J. (2002). Social Work: Gender, Care and Justice. *British Journal of Social Work*, 32(6): 799–814.

Orr, S. (2011). Reimagining Global Climate Change: Alternatives to the UN Treaty Process. *Global Environmental Politics*, 11 (4): 134–138. Available at https://www.mitpressjournals.org/doi/abs/10.1162/GLEP_r_00087?journalCode=glep, accessed on 12.12.2018.

Otto, H. and W. Lorenz (1999). Editorial, *European Journal of Social Work*, 2(1): 1–2.

Padgett, D. K. (2016). *Qualitative Methods in Social Work Research* (Vol. 36). Los Angeles: Sage Publications.

Parel, A. (1997). *Hind Swaraj and Other Writings of M.K. Gandhi*. Cambridge: Cambridge University Press.

Patel, R. and J. Moore (2017). *A History of the World in Seven Cheap Things*. California: University of California Press.

Pawar, M. (2014). Social work practice with local communities in developing countries: Imperatives for political engagement, *Sage Open*: 1–11. Available at http://journals.sagepub.com/doi/pdf/10.1177/2158244014538640, accessed on 12.12.2017.

Pawar, M., R. Sheridan and H. Georgina (2004). International Social Work Practicum in India, *Australian Social Work*, 57(3): 223–36.

Payne, M. (1997). *Modern Social Work Theory*. Basingstoke: Palgrave Macmillan.

Payne, M. (2005). *The Origins of Social Work: Continuity and Change*. Basingstoke: Palgrave Macmillan.

Payne, M. (2006). International Social Work Research and Health Inequalities, *Journal of Comparative Social Welfare*, 22(2): 115–24.

Payne, M. and G.A. Askeland (2008). *Globalization and International Social Work: Postmodern Change and Challenge*. Farnham: Ashgate.

Pease, B. (2010). *Undoing Privilege: Unearned Advantage in a Divided World*. London: Zed Books.

Penhale B. (1999) Research on elder abuse: Lessons for practice. In Eastman M. & Slater P. (eds) *Elder Abuse: Critical issues in policy and practice*. London: Age Concern Books: 1–23.

Penhale, B., J. Parker and P. Kingston (2000). *Elder Abuse: Approaches to Working with Violence*. Birmingham: Venture Press.

Peri, K., J. Fanslow and J. Hand (2009). Keeping Older People Safe by Preventing Elder Abuse and Neglect, *Social Policy Journal of New Zealand*, 35: 159–72.

Phelan, A. (2008). Elder Abuse, Ageism, Human Rights and Citizenship: Implications for Nursing Discourse, *Nursing Inquiry*, 15(4): 320–29.

Philip, D. and M. Reisch (2015). Rethinking Social Work's Interpretation of 'Environmental Justice': From Local to Global, *Social Work Education*, 34(5): 471–83.

Pinkerton, J. and J. Campbell (2002). Social Work and Social Justice in Northern Ireland, Towards a New Occupational Space, *British Journal of Social Work*, 32: 723–37.

Pittaway, E. and L. Bartolomei (2005). Woman to Woman: A Gender Sensitive Response to Tsunami Affected Women, Training Report (January). Available online at: http://www.crr.unsw.edu.au, accessed 17.05.2006.

Pittaway, E., L. Bartolomei and S. Rees (2007). Gendered Dimensions of the 2004 Tsunami and a Potential Social Work Response in Post-Disaster Situations, *International Social Work*, 50(3): 307–19.

Popple, K. (2015). *Analysing Community Work: Theory and Practice*, 2nd edn. Maidenhead: Open University Press.

Powell, J. and J. Robinson (2007). The 'International Dimension' in Social Work Education: Current Developments in England, *European Journal of Social Work*, 10: 383–99.

Powell, M. and A. Barrientos (2004). Welfare Regimes and the Welfare Mix, *European Journal of Political Research*, 43: 83–105.

Pritchard, J. (1999). Good Practice: Victims' Perspectives. In J. Pritchard (ed.), *Elder Abuse Work: Best Practice in Britain and Canada*. London: Jessica Kingsley, Chapter 8.

Ranta-Tyrkkö, S. (2014). Out of sight, out of mind? The mining industry in the peripheral regions of Finland and Odisha, Eastern India. In K. Loftsdóttir & L. Jensen (2016). *Crisis in the Nordic Nations and Beyond. At the Intersection of Environment, Finance and Multiculturalism*. London: Ashgate: 101–120.

Reamer, F. (2013). *Social Work Values and Ethics*. New York: Columbia University Press.

Rees, S., E. Pittaway and L. Bartolomei (2005). Waves of Violence: Women in Post-Tsunami Sri Lanka, *Australasian Journal of Disaster and Trauma Studies*. Available online at: http://www.massey.ac.nz/trauma/issues/2005-2/rees.htm, accessed on 12.12.2017.

Roberts, D. (2002). *Shattered Bonds: The Color of Child Welfare*. New York: Basic Books.

Rose, S.J. and W. Meezan (1996). Variations in Perceptions of Child Neglect, *Child Welfare*, 75(2): 139–60.

Sanders, E. (2009). Fleeing drought in the Horn of Africa. *Los Angeles Times*, 25.10.2009.

Schmitz, C.L., T. Matyók, L.M. Sloan and C. James (2012). The Relationship between Social Work and Environmental Sustainability: Implications for Interdisciplinary Practice, *International Journal of Social Welfare*, 21(3): 278–86.

Schwabe, A. (2006). New Zealand Food Help for Kenyans is for the Dogs. *Spiegel Online*, 2.2.2006. Available at http://www.spiegel.de/international/dog-food-against-famine-new-zealand-food-help-for-kenyans-is-for-the-dogs-a-398609.html, accessed on 13.12.2017.

Scourfield, Peter (2005). Direct Payments, *Working with Older People*, 9(4): 20–23.

Selener, D. (1997). *Participatory Action Research and Social Change*. The Cornell Participatory Action Research Network, New York: Cornell University.

Selman, P. (2009). The Rise and Fall of Intercountry Adoption in the 21st Century, *International Social Work*, 52(5): 575–94.

Sewpaul, V. (2005). Global Standards: Promise and Pitfalls for Re-Inscribing Social Work into Civil Society, *International Journal of Social Welfare*, 14(3): 210–17.

Shardlow, S. (2002). Values, Ethics and Social Work. In R. Adams, L. Dominelli and M. Payne (eds), *Social Work: Themes, Issues and Critical Debates*. Basingstoke: Palgrave: 30–40.

Shiva, V. (1998). The Greening of Global Reach. In G. Thuatail, S. Dalby and P. Routledge (eds), *The Geopolitics Reader*. London and New York: Routledge: 230–143.

Smith, C.J. and G. Hugo (2008). Migration, Urbanization, and the Spread of Sexually Transmitted Diseases: Empirical and Theoretical Observations in China and Indonesia. In J.R. Logan (ed.), *Urban China in Transition*, Oxford: Blackwell Publishing: 294–314.

Smith, R. (2008). *Social Work and Power*. Basingstoke: Palgrave Macmillan.

Spandler, H. (2004). Friend or Foe? Towards a Critical Assessment of Direct Payments, *Critical Social Policy*, 24(2): 187–209.

Spandler, H. and N. Vick (2006). Opportunities for Independent Living Using Direct Payments in Mental Health, *Health and Social Care in the Community*, 14(2): 107–15.

Stasiulis, D. (2008). Revisiting the Permanent Temporary Labour Migration Dichotomy. In C. Gabriel and H. Pellerin (eds), *Governing International Labour Migration: Current Issues, Challenges and Dilemmas*, Oxon/New York: Routledge: 95–111.

Statham, O.C.J. (2009). *Disproportionality in Child Welfare: The Prevalence of Black and Minority Ethnic Children within the 'Looked After' and Children in Need Populations and on Child Protection Registers in England*. Department for Children, London: Schools and Families.

Stocker, L. and Kennedy D. (2009). Cultural Models of the Coast of Australia: Toward Sustainability. *Coastal Management*, 37(5): 387–404.

Stonehouse, B. (1992). Adoption law in Australia, Australian Institute for Family Studies, No. 1. ISSN 1038-0507, ISBN 0 642 17350 8. Available at https://aifs.gov.au/sites/default/files/publication-documents/adoption_law_in_australia.pdf, accessed on 23.08.2018.

Tamburro, A. (2013). Including Decolonization in Social Work Education and Practice, *Journal of Indigenous Social Development*, 2(1): 1–16.

Taylor, B. and M. Donnelly (2006). Professional Perspectives on Decision Making about the Longterm Care of Older People, *British Journal of Social Work*, 36(5): 807–26.

Taylor, B.J. (2006). Risk Management Paradigms in Health and Social Services for Professional Decision Making on the Long-Term Care of Older People, *British Journal of Social Work*, 36(8): 1187–207.

Tew, J. (2006). Understanding Power and Powerlessness: Towards a Framework for Emancipatory Practice in Social Work, *Journal of Social Work*, 6(1): 33–51.

Thompson, N. (2016). *Anti-discriminatory Practice: Equality, Diversity and Social Justice* (Practice social work series). London/New York: Palgrave Macmillan.

Thorne, B. (2009). Childhood: Changing and Dissonant Meanings, *International Journal of Learning and Media*, 1(1): 19–27.

Timonen, V., J. Convery and S. Cahill (2006). Care Revolutions in the Making? A Comparison of Cash-For-Care Programmes in Four European Countries, *Ageing and Society*, 26: 455–74.

Tower, C.C. (1996). *Understanding Child Abuse and Neglect*, 3rd edn. Boston, MA: Allyn & Bacon.

Trevithick, P. (2005). *Social Work Skills: A Practice Handbook*. Berkshire: Open University Press.

Tuhiwai Smith, L. (1999). *Decolonizing Methodologies: Research and Indigenous Peoples*. London and New York: Zed Books.

Turner, B.S. (1986). *Equality*. London: Tavistock.

Uhlenberg, P. (1996). Intergenerational support in Sri Lanka: the elderly and their children. In T.K. Hareven (ed.), *Aging and Generational Relations Over the Life Course*. Berlin: de Gruyter, Polity Press: 462–82.

United Nations (1994). *Human Rights and Social Work: A Manual for Schools of Social Work and the Social Work Profession*. Professional Series 1. Geneva: UN.

UN Office of the Special Envoy for Tsunami Recovery (UNSETR) (2005a). Statistics. Available at: www.tsunamispecialenvoy.org/country/srilank.asp, accessed 12.12.2017.

UNFPA (2005). Human Rights Principles. UNFPA. Available at: http://www.unfpa.org/resources/human-rights-principles, accessed 18.12.2018.

Ungerson, C. (2004). Whose Empowerment and Independence? A Cross-National Perspective on 'Cash for Care' Schemes, *Ageing Society*, 24: 189–212.

UNHCR (2013). *War's Human Cost: Global Trends 2013*. Geneva: United Nations High Commission for Refugees.

UNSETR (2005b). *Implications for Women*. Available online at: www.tsunami specialenvoy.org/briefs/impactonwomen.asp, accessed 12.12.2017.

UNSETR (2005c). *Human Rights and Tsunami Recovery*. Available online at:www.tsunamispecialenvoy.org/briefs/humanrights.asp, accessed 12.12.2017.

USA Today (2017). Hijab becomes symbol of resistance, feminism in the age of Trump. *USA Today* 15.3.2017. Available at https://www.usatoday.com/story/news/nation-now/2017/03/15/hijab-becomes-symbol-resistance-feminism-age-trump/98475212/, accessed 4.7.2017.

van Bavel, M., K. Janssens, W. Schakenraad and N. Thurlings (2010). *Elder Abuse in Europe: Background and Position Paper*. Utrecht, The Netherlands: MOVISIE, Netherlands Centre for Social Development.

Vasak, K. (1977). Human Rights: A Thirty-Year Struggle: The Sustained Efforts to give Force of Law to the Universal Declaration of Human Rights, *UNESCO Courier* 30:11. Paris: United Nations Educational, Scientific, and Cultural Organization.

Vertovec, S. (2001). Transnationalism and Identity, *Journal of Ethnic and Migration Studies*, 27 (4). doi:10.1080/13691830120090386.

Wade, R.H. (2003). Is Globalization Reducing Poverty and Inequality?, *World Development*, 32(4): 567–89.

Waites, M. (2005). *The Age of Consent: Young People, Sexuality and Citizenship*. Basingstoke: Palgrave Macmillan.

Waldman, A. (2001). *A Nation Challenged: Resistance; Behind the Burka: Women Subtly Fought Taliban, The New York Times*, 19.11.2001. Available at http://www.nytimes.com/2001/11/19/world/a-nation-challenged-resistance-behind-the-burka-women-subtly-fought-taliban.html, accessed 4.07.2017.

Walsh, T., G. Wilson and E. O'Connor (2010). Local European and Global: An Exploration of Migrations of Social Workers into Ireland, *British Journal of Social Work*, 40(6): 1978–95.

Weaver, H.N. (1999). Indigenous People and the Social Work Profession: Defining Culturally Competent Services, *Social Work*, 44(3): 217–25.

Webb, S. (2003). Local Orders and Global Chaos in Social Work, *European Journal of Social Work*, 6(2): 191–204.

Wehbi, S. (2009). Deconstructing Motivations: Challenging International Social Work Placements, *International Social Work*, 52(1): 48–59.

Weiss, I., J. Gal and J. Dixon (2003). *Professional Ideologies and Preferences in Social Work: A Global Study*. Westport, CT: Praeger Publishers.

Weiss, I. and P. Welbourneeds. (2007). *Social Work as a Profession – a Comparative Cross-National Perspective*. Birmingham: IASSW/Venture Press.

Wells, K. (2012). Making Gender and Generation: Between the Local and the Global in Africa. In A. Tsum-Danso and R. Ame (eds), *Childhood at the Intersection of the Local and the Global*. London: Palgrave Macmillan: 143–59.

Whitbourne, S.K. and J.R. Sneeed (2002). The Paradox of Well-Being, Identity Processes, and Stereotype Threat: Ageism and Its Potential Relationships to the Self in Later Life. In D. Todd, *Ageism: Stereotyping and Prejudice against Older Persons*, Cambridge: Mamit Press: 247–273.

WHO (2002). *World report on violence and health: Summary*. Geneva: World Health Organization. Available at http://www.who.int/violence_injury_prevention/violence/world_report/en/summary_en.pdf, accessed on 13.12.2017.

WHO (2011). *European report on preventing elder maltreatment*. Copenhagen: World Health Organization. Available at http://www.euro.who.int/__data/assets/pdf_file/0010/144676/e95110.pdf, accessed on 13.12.2017.

WHO (2014). *Female Genital Mutilation: Factsheet*. Geneva: World Health Organization. Available at http://apps.who.int/iris/bitstream/handle/10665/112328/WHO_RHR_14.12_eng.pdf;jsessionid=820A8E3F67CB340806FB4CC4F7B98597?sequence=1, accessed on 14.12.2018.

WHO (2016). *Female Genital Mutilation: Factsheet*. Geneva: World Health Organization. Available at http://www.who.int/mediacentre/factsheets/fs241/en/, accessed on 12.12.2017.

WHO and INPEA (2002). Missing Voices: Views of older persons on elder abuse. World Health Organization and The International Network for the Prevention of Elder Abuse. Available at http://apps.who.int/iris/bitstream/handle/10665/67371/WHO_NMH_VIP_02.1.pdf;jsessionid=191E401D9ABBDF45D7E9D264DD84EED6?sequence=1, accessed on 3.1.2019.

Williams, P. (2006). *Social Work with People with Learning Difficulties*. Exeter: Learning Matters.

Wistow, J., L. Dominelli, K.J. Oven, C.E. Dunn and S.E. Curtis (2015). The Role of Formal and Informal Networks in Supporting Older People's Care during Extreme Weather Events, *Policy and Politics*, 43(1): 119–35.

Wood, G.G. and C.T. Tully (2006). *The Structural Approach to Direct Practice in Social Work: A Social Constructionist Perspective*. CUPOLA: Columbia University Press online.

The World Bank (2017). Unemployment, youth total (% of total labour force ages 15–24) (modelled ILO estimate). Washington: The World Bank Group. Available at https://data.worldbank.org/indicator/SL.UEM.1524.ZS, accessed on 13.12.2017.

Yegenoglu, M. (1998). *Colonial Fantasies: Towards a Feminist Reading of Orientalism*. Cambridge: Cambridge University Press.

Youth Policy (2014). Factsheet: Kenya. Available at http://www.youthpolicy.org/factsheets/country/kenya/, accessed on 12.12.2014.

Index

Note: Page numbers with *f* indicate figures.

discrimination
  of aboriginal families and cultures, 47
  cultural competence and, 25
  diversity work and, 51, 56, 59, 60, 64
  environmental exploitation and, 89
  gender, 56, 74
  human rights and, 18, 64
  medical model and, 60
  otherness and, 51
  positive discrimination policies for
    marginalised groups, 59
  power and, 20, 21
  structural work and, 74
  sustainability work and, 89
diversity work, 50–66
  abilities and recognising diversity,
    60–63
  cultural diversity and, 54
  defined, 50–53
  difference in, 50–61, 53*f*
  disabilities in UK, RoI, and Australia
    (example), 61–63
  dominance in, 51
  equality in, 50, 51–52, 53, 53*f*
  gender and, 57–60
  gender blindness and disaster aid
    in Thailand, Indonesia, and Sri
    Lanka (example), 58–60
  human rights and cultural practices
    in UK, Africa and South Asia
    (example), 64–65
  human rights in, 63–65
  inclusiveness in, 53, 53*f*, 59
  othering in, 50–51
  power and privilege in, 53*f*
  religious diversity and, 54–57
  religious diversity in Europe
    (example), 55–57
  social justice in, 50, 51–52, 53*f*, 63, 65
  summary of, 53*f*
domestic violence (DV), 27, 31, 68, 79

education. *See* social work education
elder abuse in RoI and UK (example),
    35–38
empowerment, structural work and,
    78–80

environment. *See also* sustainability work
  environmental exploitation in
    Finland and India (example),
    89–90
  social work education and, 85
  social work research on exploitation, 90
  sustainability work and, 88–90
Europe
  migration and refugees in, 98–100
  religious diversity in, 55–57
examples of global mindedness in
    practice
  adoption for seeking permanency
    for children in need, global,
    46–48
  aid in Kenya, failed or faulty, 91–93
  child labour in Ghana and Bolivia,
    77–78
  community development in
    Mozambique, 94–97
  disabilities in UK, RoI, and Australia,
    61–63
  elder abuse in RoI and UK, 35–38
  environmental exploitation in
    Finland and India, 89–90
  gender blindness and disaster aid
    in Thailand, Indonesia, and Sri
    Lanka, 58–60
  human rights and cultural practices
    in UK, Africa and South Asia,
    64–65
  Indigenous practices in New
    Zealand, practice work and, 39–41
  local activism *versus* global
    dominance in India, 75–76
  migration and refugees in European
    countries, 98–100
  religious diversity in Europe, 55–57
  self-help groups in Bangladesh and
    India, 79–80
  social workers in India and UK,
    differing roles of, 42–45
  women's contribution to crafting
    communities in Australia, older,
    81–84
  youth policy in Kenya, comparative,
    71–74

Family Group Conference (FGC), 38–41, 65
Finland, environmental exploitation in, 89–90
first generation human rights, 18
Fry, Elizabeth, 4

gender
  blindness and disaster aid in Thailand, Indonesia, and Sri Lanka (example), 58–60
  diversity work and, 57–60
Ghana, child labour in, 77–78
global in social work practice, defined, 16
globalisation and international social work, 8–12
  global problems and, 9–11
  global solutions and, 11–12
global mindedness
  borders and, pushing, 101–3
  as bridging theory, 12–13
  defining, 16
  diversity work and, 50–66
  knowledge and, 22f, 23–25
  in practice, 15, 101–9 (*See also* international social work)
  practice skills and, 22f, 25–28
  professional practice and, 103–5, 104f
  in protection work, 31–49
  in research, 105–7
  research and education and, 103–5
  in social work education, 108
  in structural work, 67–84
  in sustainability work, 85–100
  themes in, 16–22, 17f, 19f
  in theory building, 107–8
  values and, 22–23, 22f
glocal, 16–17
group work, 27

history
  of international social work, 4–5
  structural work and, 76–78
human rights, 17f, 18–20
  cultural practices in UK, Africa and South Asia and (example), 64–65

in diversity work, 63–65
in protection work, 45–48
Human Rights Convention (HRC), 41, 55

India, 5, 6, 9, 10, 39, 58, 59, 67, 71, 91
  environmental exploitation in, 89–90
  local activism *versus* global dominance in, 75–76
  self-help groups in, 79–80
  social workers in, differing roles of, 42–45
Indigenous practices in New Zealand, practice work and (example), 39–41
Indonesia, gender blindness and disaster aid in, 58–60
inequality
  among older people, 83
  diversity work and, 50, 52, 54, 57–58, 64
  environmental exploitation and, 90
  gender, 57–58, 64
  globalisation and, 9
  policy reform and, 71
  power and, 21
  religion and, 54
  research and, 106
  social development and, 90, 92, 94
  structural work and, 9, 67, 68, 71, 74, 83
  sustainability work and, 88, 90
  technology and, 88
intergenerational relations, structural work and, 81–84
International Association of Schools of Social Work (IASSW), 2, 5, 12
International Council on Social Welfare (ICSW), 5
International Federation of Social Work (IFSW), 2, 5
  Global Agenda for Social Work and Social Development, 85
international organisations (INGOs), 94, 96
international social work, 1–14, 101–19

bridging theory and, 12–13
defining, 2–3, 50
globalisation and, 8–12
historical understanding of, 4–5
human rights and, 17*f*, 18–20
internationalisation of social work
    today, 5–6
knowledge in, 22*t*, 23–25
local–global–local (L–G–L)
    perspectives and, 16–18, 17*f*, 19*f*
opportunities in, 7–8
power and, 17*f*, 20–22
practice skills and, 22*t*, 25–28
professional, 103–5
in protection work, 31–49
roles within, 103–8, 104*f*
self-reflection in, 105
in sustainability work, 85–100
values in, 22–23, 22*f*
without borders, 101–3

Kenya
    aid in, failed or faulty, 91–93
    youth policy in, comparative, 71–74
knowledge for global mindedness, 22*f*,
    23–25
    Indigenous knowledge, 24
    scientific knowledge, 23–24

LGBT (Lesbian Gay Bisexual Trans)
    communities, 51
local activism *versus* global dominance
    in India (example), 75–76
local–global–local (L–G–L) perspectives,
    16–18, 17*f*, 19*f*
local in social work practice, defined, 16

medical model, 60
Middle Eastern refugees, 98–100
migration and refugees in European
    countries (example), 98–100
Millennium Development Goals of
    the United Nations, 70–71
Missing Voices report, 35
Mozambique, community
    development in, 94–97
Muslim women, 55–57

National Alliance of People's
    Movements (NAPM), 75
National Centre for the Protection of
    Older People, 36
New Zealand, Indigenous practices in,
    39–41
non-governmental organisations
    (NGOs), 43, 79, 91, 103
Northern Ireland (NI) model of service
    provision, 35
No Secrets report, 36

Older Peoples Experiences of
    Mistreatment and Abuse, 35
oppression, 11, 13, 15, 103, 107, 109
    antisemitism and, 102
    diversity work and, 50, 51, 55–57,
        63, 65
    dominance and, 51
    empowerment and, 78
    environmental exploitation and, 89
    familial or patriarchal, 56
    human rights and, 63, 65
    of indigenous communities, 69
    knowledge and, 25
    power and, 20–21, 70
    structural work and, 67, 68, 69, 70, 78
    sustainability work and, 89
    of women, 55–57
othering, 50–51
others, problems of, 7

participatory learning action, 95
participatory rural appraisal (PRA), 95
Patkar, Medha, 75–76
patriarchy, 57
policy. *See* social policy
power
    in building global mindedness, 17*f*,
        20–22
    in diversity work, 53*f*
    structural work and, 69–70
practice skills, for global mindedness,
    22*f*, 25–28
praxis, 11, 18, 25, 101, 104, 107
professional practice and global
    mindedness, 103–5, 104*f*